D0373148

WORSHIP IN THE WAY OF THE CROSS

LEADING WORSHIP FOR THE SAKE OF OTHERS

JOHN FREDERICK

IVP Books

An imprint of InterVarsity Press
Downers Grove, Illinois

InterVarsity Press
P.O. Box 1400, Downers Grove, IL 60515-1426
ivpress.com
email@ivpress.com

InterVarsity Press® is the book-publishing division of InterVarsity Christian Fellowship/USA®, a movement of students and faculty active on campus at hundreds of universities, colleges, and schools of nursing in the United States of America, and a member movement of the International Fellowship of Evangelical Students. For information about local and regional activities, visit intervarsity.org.

Scripture quotations, unless otherwise noted, are from The Holy Bible, English Standard Version, copyright © 2001 by Crossway Bibles, a division of Good News Publishers. Used by permission. All rights reserved.

While any stories in this book are true, some names and identifying information may have been changed to protect the privacy of individuals.

Cover design: Cindy Kiple
Interior design: Jeanna Wiggins
Images: © stellalevi/iStockphoto

ISBN 978-0-8308-4488-3 (print)
ISBN 978-0-8308-9184-9 (digital)

Printed in the United States of America ♾

Library of Congress Cataloging-in-Publication Data
A catalog record for this book is available from the Library of Congress.

P	22	21	20	19	18	17	16	15	14	13	12	11	10	9	8	7	6	5	4	3	2	1
Y	35	34	33	32	31	30	29	28	27	26	25	24	23	22	21	20	19	18	17			

For Tara, Liam, and Zoe

CONTENTS

PREFACE AND ACKNOWLEDGMENTS

Worship in the way of the cross involves restructuring, reimagining, and renewing the world both in the image of the God who is love and through the embodiment of love by God's people, the church. For the better part of the past decade I have been studying this concept in the Bible and in the writings of theologians of the church through the ages. Experiencing the truth of this theology in real life in the church is, however, a more recent event. In fact, my experience with the church, like the experience of many others, has been a mixed bag of joy and frustration. In what can only be described as the extreme, providential irony of God, I write this preface to a book that exalts the church as the means by which the world encounters the transforming love of Jesus Christ after having come out of a season of a schism in leadership in what proved to be a really unhealthy and soul-crushing church situation. I'm now in the midst of beginning a new work with a group of friends, which I hope will embody the reconciling and redemptive love of God in Jesus Christ to all people.

I share this because it is part of my story. It is important for me to be "on the level" with you, the reader, as I write what could appear to be an idealistic treatise of hope and wonder at what the church is and what the church can become through God's gracious provision and spiritual power. I believe in the transformative power of Christ's love and presence through the church to a certain extent in spite of—not because of—many of my past experiences in the church. In all of my church experiences (even my most recent, negative experience), there have been glimpses of redemptive beauty. This is so even while dealing with the persistent irritation of ecclesially inflicted wounds resulting from problems in some churches to which I have belonged.

My experience at Park Street Church in Boston stands out as the tipping point for me where a specific theology of the church, the church as the worshiping community in which Christ's transformative presence resides through his people, became more than an abstract idea but a tangible, lived reality. Without idealizing my brief experience at Park Street, I will say that it was the first place I fully experienced the theology I had studied about and dreamed about. My time there was so profoundly life-giving and spiritually refreshing. It took me two years to really let go of my vital connection to that church after moving twenty-six hundred miles across the country to take up my current post as an assistant professor. There were other churches along the way that contributed to the lived experience of the love of Christ in the church. Some of these (but not all) also weaved those glimpses of hope with theological ideas and an ecclesial praxis that virtually crushed my faith in the gospel.

Yet here is the profound paradox: the burden-bearing of the church is—as Paul discusses in his epistles—the means by which we embody the love of Christ; in and through his loving community, the church, we have the potential to become like the God who is love. Thus even the church in its imperfection (including my negative experiences, while definitely regrettable and unfortunate) does not negate a theology of the primacy and importance of the church; rather, it validates it! If bearing the burden of the other were an easy task, it would not actually be a burden to bear. Even the most diligent, loving church communities will fall short. Yet this is not only a picture of the inevitability of sin; it is the means by which God, through our love for the other and our experience of being loved by the other, transforms us into the others-centered, self-giving image of his divine love. The enactment and reception of this burden-bearing love is the way we become like the God whose love is displayed, unveiled, explicated, and experienced in the cross of Jesus Christ. In other words, we experience a growth in Christlike character through the community of Christ's love, the church, which results in our spiritual transformation into the perfect image of God's love. It is toward this task that God calls us so that we might be a people who—by embodying his love—become reconciled reconcilers and agents of his love and peace in this beautiful, terrible world.[1]

As we begin, I wish to extend thanks and genuine appreciation to a host of people who, through their support and friendship along the way, have helped this book come into existence. The pride of place goes to my wife, Tara, who has faithfully traveled with me through many career paths and across many continents as my deepest companion and most genuine, beloved confidant. Without her resolve we would never have stayed the course to finish my doctoral studies in Scotland. I received several job offers in other fields while studying abroad, but because of her strength of character and her perseverance of spirit, I was convinced that staying and finishing the course was the right thing to do. Without her, I would have convinced myself that doing a PhD was crazy (which it is) and quit. I was so impressed at her ability to get a job so quickly in the UK, which was essentially what allowed us to keep from sinking financially during those doctoral years. Truly, this book would never have been parsed out if it weren't for her work. The fact that we were and are a team made my work on this project possible. I also wish to apologize to her for making a habit during those years of hijacking our dinner conversations to talk about whatever incredibly boring theological minutiae I had recently discovered. Most of all, I am grateful for the warmth and authenticity of her soul. It is my greatest joy to enjoy the seemingly simple but deeply profound spiritual moments of life with her: listening to records, playing with Zoe and Liam, and enjoying a cup of coffee or a meal. To live life with the person I most admire and who reminds me most of the power of selfless, self-giving love is my greatest privilege and joy.

Thanks and love to my family: Carole, John D, Joel, Jackie, and to all of my extended family and relatives for your support of me, and for always supporting my musical and academic endeavors even when that included sitting through loud ska concerts and my phase as a raging, immature Bible thumper. Special thanks to Auntie Diana (AKA "Tia") for her presence, love, and support for Tara, the kids, and me. Your hospitality and humility is a source of familial warmth and Christlike encouragement to us.

I am grateful to Matthew Kruse at Seven Mile Road church for his personal mentoring and his support of my seminary education during some crucial early years of my faith. Likewise, the early influence of Msgr. Paul Garrity, Fr. Tim Kearney, and Fr. Mike Ferraro provided pastoral and

formative experiences that instilled in me a love for social justice ministries and the liturgical Great Tradition of the church. I'm incredibly
thankful to Rev. Roger Nelson for his friendship, for his support for the
local music scene in Boston, and for his ministry during his time at St.
John's Episcopal Church in Saugus, Massachusetts. I am glad that I had
the opportunity to work at Park Street Church in Boston with the entire
staff and congregation, especially Gordon Hugenberger, Walter Kim, and
Damon Addleman. Among my Anglican brothers and sisters, I am
grateful for the spiritual guidance of Bishop William Murdoch and for
the early mentoring of Fr. Sam Schutz. All of the clergy, congregations,
and people of the Anglican Diocese in New England hold a special place
in my story and heart. I'm very grateful to T. C. Moore and Chris
Llewellyn for their contributions to this book.

In the world of the academy, many thanks go to Dr. Grant Macaskill,
who supervised my PhD thesis at the University of St. Andrews. Thanks
as well to N. T. Wright, Mark Elliot, and Scott Hafemann for giving me
the privilege of coediting a book (*Galatians and Christian Theology*) with
such luminaries. I would be remiss if I didn't directly thank Dr. Michael
Gorman, who I consider to be one of the great Pauline scholars of the
church. Dr. Gorman was kind enough to read my entire PhD thesis and
to offer extended, valuable feedback. His work on cruciformity has been
highly influential on me and on many others, and I hope that the present
work contributes something to the conversation in which he is the
leading voice.

Thanks go as well to Dr. Jason Hiles, Anna Faith Smith, and the faculty
of the College of Theology at Grand Canyon University and Grand
Canyon Theological Seminary. Special thanks and appreciation are due
my friends, colleagues, and students in the Center for Worship Arts and
the GCU College of Theology. I greatly appreciate the catalytic and creative foundational work of Scott Fehrenbacher and Bart Millard. Likewise,
I'm grateful for the collegiality, collaborative spirit, and expert skill of my
colleagues Eric Johnson and John McJunkin in the GCU Recording
Studio, Mark Huggins in the College of Fine Arts and Production, and
my friend and colleague Jonathan Sharpe, and my friend and colleague
Jonathan Sharpe. Your support across the board has helped to encourage

me, to shape my thought, and to refine my theology. Of course, any mistakes or missteps that remain in this book belong solely to me.

Last, I am sincerely thankful to the editorial team and the entire staff at InterVarsity Press. Special thanks go to the editors of this book whose feedback has been substantive and very helpful. In particular, I would like to thank Al Hsu for providing not only a wonderful and efficient editorial experience but also an educational experience. His editorial insights and direction have no doubt helped me to grow as a writer, and I am very grateful for his commitment to this project.

As we begin, let us reflect and pray together about the glory of the triune God: Father, Son, and Holy Spirit, by contemplatively praying this ancient prayer of the church:

"Glory to God (Gloria in excelsis)"

Glory to God in the highest,
and peace to his people on earth.
Lord God, heavenly King,
almighty God and Father,
we worship you, we give you thanks,
we praise you for your glory.
Lord Jesus Christ, only Son of the Father,
Lord God, Lamb of God,
you take away the sin of the world:
have mercy on us;
you are seated at the right hand of the Father:
receive our prayer.
For you alone are the Holy One,
you alone are the Lord,
you alone are the Most High,
Jesus Christ,
with the Holy Spirit,
in the glory of God the Father. Amen.[2]

PART 1

THE STORY THAT SHAPES CRUCIFORM WORSHIP

THE STORIES THAT TRANSFORM
(OR DEFORM) US AND THE WORLD

The Narrative Background to Cruciform Worship

I often begin theological discussions with (typically zany) stories. This is not merely because I enjoy placing random reflections and observations about the weird and absurd side by side with rigorous and serious discussions about God and life (although that is true as well). Rather, it is because I think that through the mechanisms of anecdote, laughter, and empathy, one can enter into the task of constructive theology in ways that are both more robustly human and more deeply evocative and explicative of the divine. By telling stories, we are able to discover the implications and coherence of our various thoughts about life, ethics, and God. This process of reading and telling stories is particularly effective for raising questions that sometimes lead to theological tensions. These tensions, however, are not necessarily negative, causing us emotional discomfort or debilitating doubt. Rather, they function as the eyeglasses of grace, helping believers and the church to avoid placing a theological muzzle over the mouth of God's voice in Scripture.[1]

Story is not just an effective means of conveying ideas in the form of an illustration. Rather, story itself creates an encounter which affects reality. For Christians this encounter is an encounter with God himself by the power of the Holy Spirit. The story of Scripture is not meant merely to communicate a set of facts about God to us in a purely abstract sense. The point of the gospel story of Jesus Christ is something much more profound than the compilation of random theological facts. In the story of the gospel we experience God and we encounter God as a person in whom and through whom and with whom we discover not only who he is but who we are in him. Story—and in particular, the true story of the gospel—helps us to encounter God so that we might know who we are becoming in and through communion with God and each other.[2] We don't tell and engage with stories because we already understand; rather, we engage in narrative-dwelling and storytelling so that we might understand. In this sense, revelation can happen through story.

The point of the anecdote that follows is to introduce us to the central thesis of this book: namely, that through knowing and living out the story of Jesus Christ in life and worship, we are transformed by his love so that we might transform the world through his love. Unique among the countless other myths, tales, and narratives of this world, the gospel invites us into a way of life that is paradoxically founded upon an instrument of death, the cross. As we consider what it means to lead in worship and to encounter God through worship, we must focus on this very paradox: the one story that has the power to redeem all things, to reconcile all peoples, and to restore everlasting peace is the story of a God whose power is defined not by the terrible fierceness of a warlord or the brute force of a tyrant but by the vulnerability of a baby in a manger and the humility of a carpenter on a cross. The gospel is not a story instead of every other story. It is not the only story. Rather, the gospel is the victorious story about the God who defeats the inevitable (though sometimes unspoken or ignored) tragic element of every other story—namely, sin and death. It is the story of a God who wins the victory not through the violence of an army but through the vulnerability of the cross and the vindication of the resurrection. Worship in the way of the cross is thus much more than a style or approach to worship; it is a transformative participation in the redemptive, reconciling love of Jesus Christ.

The Intrusion of Sin into the Park of Peace:
A Case Study in Toddler Liturgies

"Announcement time!" shouted Juan in the loudest voice a five-year old could muster up, "I have an announcement to make!" *What's this now? An announcement?* I thought to myself, *Hmmm, what public notification shall he declare to us?* Though previously engaged in an epic quest to reach the top of the jungle gym, the likes of which no toddler in history had ever dared to attempt (in his mind at least), my two-year old son Liam was instantly drawn by the sound of Juan's loud declaration. Thus we decided to postpone our Everest-like voyage to the top of toddler-earth to investigate the proposed speech. The climb would have to wait for another time, perhaps after the juice box and peanut-butter cracker segment of the journey (AKA, snack time).[3] After all, Juan had an announcement to make!

Racing toward the center of the park, Liam and every other curious recipient of the "Juanian playground pre-announcement declaration of forthcoming proclamation" sensed that a happening was about to occur. Now, Juan (who was clearly the alpha male among the park dwellers present on that particular day) momentarily withheld the announcement as he stood with an almost stoic, presidential poise in his Teenage Mutant Ninja Turtles T-shirt awaiting the flock of hungry pre-kindergarten sheep who were approaching his majesty with great expectation for the impending, yet still undefined and somewhat ambiguous ruckus. However, it wasn't merely Juan's charismatic presence that contributed to the success of his soon-to-be speech. Rather, the ubiquitous efficacy of his pre-oration declaration can also be attributed to the fact that he had spent the prior seven minutes beating a variety of children senseless over the head with a thin yet toddlerly terrifying twig.

As the last segment of toddler zombies and kindergarten cretins drew near to Juan, the group coalesced into a gestalt of mucus and mulch, characterized by an assortment of dried boogers clinging to the rims of neglected nostrils like Grandma's broken Christmas lights dangling from a dilapidated porch in the middle of July in the badlands of some metaphorical forgotten snot village in New England. The air reeked of dirty diapers and cotton candy, a disgusting mix that wafted through the atmosphere like the odorific epitome of the antithesis of freshness in-carnated in the Platonic form of the worst stench ever known to man.

"I have an announcement!" shouted Juan for the third time, this time with an air of finality that cut through the now-polluted actual air of this duly diapered and captivated crowd. At this point my son was fully en-gaged and completely committed to whatever might occur. He had, however, no idea what was actually going on. Still, he wanted in.

"Dada, Dada!" said Liam pointing at his feet, "it's shoes. And I like trucks."

"Indeed, my son," I responded, "Footwear and vehicles are super cool," laughing at the randomness of his observations as we awaited the big announcement.

And then, just like that, Juan trumpeted his declaration, and I quote: "Janie smells like bum bum undies and she is the poopy Queen."

The crowd gasped at the revelation, nay better, the potty prophecy of Juan, responding with their own participatory jests and improvisational utterances, practically all of which revolved around the classic and uni-versally laugh-inducing theme of poo. The masses (seven children and a few supervising adults) turned to Janie with great expectation to observe her response. "I am not the bum bum undies, but you are Mr. Toilet Paper." Yes! The response was both original and humorous.

Liam, perplexed by the entire ordeal, proceeded to suggest another completely nonsensical solution to the predicament. "Shoes! Shoes!" he shouted enthusiastically, thus returning to his previously established random motif of footwear. Admittedly, this was a tangential comment especially given the now obvious toilet-themed direction of the conver-sation. Yet it did still manage to bring a measure of variety to the table.

Immediately, behold![4] The crowd dispersed and a new horde of kids ran up to Liam. Raising up realistic looking toy guns, they pointed them directly at his head and shouted, "Bang, Bang, Bang, You're dead! You're dead. Die! You're dead!"

Liam was impressed by the amount of attention given to him by the horde. He was, however, completely oblivious to the fact that he had become the unarmed victim in the children's game of Hide and Go Kill. Smiling warmly, he replied with awe and joy, "Hello! Hi!"

Bewildered and annoyed, the older boys dispersed after realizing that their imaginary weapons had proven themselves to be completely ineffective against the mind of an individual not yet poisoned by the myth of redemptive violence.

The Truth of the Gospel vs. the Myth of Redemptive Violence

This myth of redemptive violence referred to above constitutes the narrative that theologian Walter Wink argues is infused into our children through the "roughly thirty-six thousand hours of television" that they consume by age eighteen. Included within this desensitizing consumption of violence through media—now intensified and multiplied by the advent of Internet video as a ubiquitous medium and, of course, video games—is the reality that average American children view "some fifteen thousand murders" during the course of their early youth and adolescence.[5] Through the absorption and assimilation of the myth that violence redeems, we initiate our children into a false reality in which the way of aggression, coercion, domination, and manipulation is actually the most successful and proper way of dealing with the ills and violence of this fallen world. This so-called gospel of the myth of redemptive violence aims not at "the unconditional love of enemies" as Jesus would have it but rather at "their final liquidation" by vengeance, violence, and the principles of retribution carried out by the power of the sword whether wielded by individuals or governments.[6] The impulse to view violence as a solution to violence—and worse, as an enjoyable recreation—resides not only in the art and media to which our children are exposed daily; it is also clearly present in the games that they play, whether virtual or physical, games like the one the plastic gunslingers played with my son that view the pretend death of a companion as a source of entertainment and joy rather than as a tragic result of sin in need of repentance and reconciliation through Christ.

While I myself participated in similar games characterized by the myth of redemptive violence as a boy and even had an entire toy chest full of pretend weapons, something changed when I became a dad. This sort of behavior is clearly make-believe and can be considered an acceptable form of beneficial performance (such as we experience, for example, in theater and screen acting). Nevertheless, when this type of play-violence was directed toward Liam on the playground that day, I found myself deeply disturbed by the make-believe murder of my son. I saw within the rules of the playground something more than an innocent game. Rather, I witnessed a demonstration of the senseless absorption into and normalization of a story, worldview, and social way of being that is contrary to the gospel narrative of the cross and resurrection of Jesus Christ.[7] At the park that day, Liam was catapulted into the foreign story and game of a world that plays by the rules of the coercive crucifiers of Rome rather than the God that Rome crucified. I was also struck by a profound paradox: the disturbing encounter was ultimately diffused through the simple innocence of a child whose ignorance in regard to the myth of redemptive violence neutralized its force and rendered it powerless by withdrawing from participation in it, thereby refusing to reciprocate its force. In the back of my mind echoed the scriptural saying of Jesus in Matthew 18:3, "Truly, I say to you, unless you turn and become like children, you will never enter the kingdom of heaven."

I wondered, *At what point was the promise of Jesus Christ to make all things new—to usher in a new kingdom in which there would be no crying, violence, sickness, or death, where we would love our enemies and pray for those who persecute us—replaced by the insidious myth that violence is inevitable, that it should be tolerated, and that it ought even to be encouraged as a form of healthy, masculine play? At what point did our theories of atonement shift to the erroneous notion that the cross is an advertisement for the acceptance and effectiveness of violence, rather than itself being the defeat and death of violence?* I longed for my son's heart to resonate with the desire to beat the weapons of this earth into plowshares to be used for gardening rather than as instruments for cultivating the practice of killing.

Conclusion: Transforming or Deforming the World Through How We Live and What We Worship

The adventure at Encanto Park ended with Liam emulating older boys as they yelled loudly and stomped on pea pods that fell from the trees surrounding the playground. The thought occurred to me as I watched my son play that day, *Life is not that much different for grown-ups and people in the church.* There are patterns, there are unspoken rules, and there are games we play that form us. I consider these patterns, rules, and games to be the formative, liturgical actions of our cultural acts of worship. The content and direction of these actions determine the object of our worship—namely, either the true and living God or something wrongly claiming that place in our lives. Our actions and the actions of others in our communities affect us by either deforming us or transforming us, but they never just leave us where we were before we entered into the life of the community. In this sense the church is not a neutral, safe, and static place whatsoever. Rather, it is a place of progress in the pursuit of a dangerous and subversive form of sanctification that involves the death of ourselves for the other so that we might find ourselves and God himself precisely through the other.[8] The stories we tell and the cultures we create—whether outside or inside the church—are enacted and received either to our destruction or to our freedom, to our alienation through isolation, or conversely to our reconciliation through Christlike participation in community and in the lives of one another.

2

THE WORLD THAT WE SHAPE AND THE WORLD THAT SHAPES US

The Transformative Power of Cruciform Worship

In chapter one, I argued that through our stories, we either transform or deform ourselves, the communities in which we live, and indeed the entire world. There I contrasted the fallen world that operates according to the myth of redemptive violence with the true story of the love of God in the person of Jesus Christ. The world invests in violence, coercion, and manipulation as the means of accomplishing its will in spite of or instead of the other. The kingdom of God as preached in the gospel presents us with another way forward, the way of God's cruciform love. The cruciform way of God in Christ is a manner of living in which every person lives and exists for the sake of the other.

CRUCIFORM WORSHIP: WORSHIP THAT FORMS US IN THE WAY OF THE CROSS

The adjective *cruciform* is a theological word used to refer to the worldview and way of life that focuses on the others-centered, self-giving love of God in the sacrificial life and death of Jesus Christ. In this book I am adopting and expanding upon the cruciform theology of Michael Gorman by applying it to the realm of worship.[1]

What does this theme of cruciformity contribute to a theology of worship? Let me explain. When God calls us to lead and live in the church, he calls us to lead and live not as lords but as servants. He calls us to model our motivations, actions, desires, and goals after the cruciform love of Jesus Christ. To be cruciform means to be conformed to the others-centered, self-giving way of the cross, the way demonstrated by Jesus himself in his humble life and death for sinners. It means seeking not to control, manipulate, intimidate, or coerce people on the basis of one's own skill, position, or prestige. Instead we are called to relinquish the desire to rule as lords, to lay down the false security and pursuit of power, to forsake the ways of the world, and therein to discover what it means to be truly and abundantly human, for the other, through love, to the glory of God. For the church and the world to be transformed into the image of the God of cruciform love, we need leaders who are themselves intentionally engaging the church and the world in worship marked by cruciform love. Further, worship itself is a means by which this cruciform love is manifested. Without the embodied, enacted cruciform love of God, the world will not meet Jesus, the world will not be changed, and the world will continue to consider "church" an irrelevant vestige of a romanticized, defunct religion now relegated to the status of a historical society or tourist attraction.

But what if we could disciple generations of worship pastors and congregants to be cruciform leaders who disciple cruciform disciples, who minister to the church in ways that help to transform the people of God— through the cruciformational ministry of the gospel of love harmonized and melodized—into a renewal in the image of God's love? What if worship pastors, who exercise a great degree of theological and spiritual influence over the church, would cease viewing themselves as artists (as opposed to theologians) but instead viewed themselves as artistic theologians? What would it look like if this ethos of cruciformity became the narrative spirituality and script of the life of the entire church? The world? This is already happening in many of our churches, and praise God! My prayer and hope is rooted in the continued cultivation and proliferation of a global, ecclesial culture of cruciform worship leading to cruciform, Christlike character among all of the congregants of the church. This must be the way forward. The church without the embodiment of the way of the cross and resurrection will never be a mechanism of transformation that ushers in the kingdom of God. Rather, it will be a museum, or worse, a mausoleum, for there is no place other than a tomb in which a religion can be placed (or disposed of) once its animating force has been removed in the name of civic unity and generic spirituality.

As we have observed in chapter one, contrary to the teachings of pop psychology and much contemporary American thought, we do not exist in this world as blank-slate individuals operating from an ahistorical, acultural place of autonomous reasoning and action. Instead, we are entangled in cultural stories, customs, rules, and social realities that precede us and that continue after we are gone; stories that shape us and stories through which we learn to become shapers of the world. But what kind of a world is shaping us, and what kind of a world are we, in turn, shaping?

Through reflecting on the social experience of a toddler in a park, it becomes apparent that the liturgies of the world are not of a singular variety but in fact coexist—often with great tension and friction—as an overlapping collage of incompatible ethical, religious, and political commitments developed and held, in many cases, at a precritical level of understanding. Sometimes these narratives overlap cohesively in commensurable ways. When this happens we can find common ground with our neighbors. More often than not, however, our narrative commitments clash. We can observe this in the various approaches and responses to violence, coercion, and justice from the stories discussed above. When friction does occur, it leaves us with at least two options. The first option is to ignore the differences in the name of a homogeneous and vacuous so-called unity. This unity seeks to pacify and placate the tension created by difference through encouraging a generic, lowest-common-denominator approach to truth and convictions. This neuters the ability of such truth or convictions to speak prophetically and powerfully in revolutionary ways that are able to transform individuals, communities, and the world. The alternative approach acknowledges the conflicting narratives and opts to live in the midst of the tension. And precisely through that good gospel tension, we experience cruciform tension, change, revolution, knowledge, and progress while injustices, lies, and false stories are brought clearly into focus and called to account.

The Christian is called to take the latter route, living into the tension created by the reconciling narrative of new creation in Christ Jesus. The question remains, however, what does any of this have to do with worship? Good question! In its fullest exposition, the inquiries raised in this chapter will have to wait until the following chapters to be fully explained. Suffice it to say here that the aim of this book is to highlight the way in which worship forms worshipers through love into the image of the God who is love. This transformational aspect to worship is not meant to operate at a merely individual level. Rather, like the communal experience of life in the park, worship that transforms us and renews us in the image of God is—through and through—a necessarily communal endeavor, guided by communal practices, truths, ethical precepts, and hopes that point to a communal eschatological goal—namely, the new heavens and the new earth. Within this community, worship leaders (and, really, all Christians) are charged with the gospel task of enacting the cruciform love of Christ to others and, conversely, receiving the cruciform love of Christ from others. When the church acts in this manner, we image and incarnate Jesus to one another in and through communal life and worship. The result of this is that we are transformed from one degree of glory to another by gazing at the glory of God in the face of Jesus Christ in one another (2 Cor 4:4-6; see also 3:18).

CONCLUSION: THE RETURN OF PEACE TO THE PARK OF GOD'S NEW CREATION

Our cultures and our communities shape us and help us to become world shapers by providing us with sets of rules, patterns of behavior, and beliefs—as evidenced by my experiences at Encanto Park. It is also the case that the park can represent a sort of "preperfection of all things by Jesus" paradigm of how community and worship are meant to function. At the same park, on the same day that my son experienced his first potty humor name-calling session and that he was the victim of his first make-believe murder, Liam and I also experienced some truly beautiful and profound realities. We saw hundreds of happy children playing youth soccer matches on the massive, open green grass fields of Encanto Park. On this beautiful, sunny, seventy-five-degree Arizona day, the smell of BBQ permeated the air, and a quick panoramic sweep of the park grounds revealed about fifty public cookouts taking place simultaneously, celebrating everything from birthdays to church group meetings to simple neighborhood gatherings. A scattering of individuals was dispersed randomly across the grassy areas bordering the sports fields, seated upon blankets, relaxing and reading books while enjoying the fresh air and the shared, open, natural space in the midst of an otherwise large, disparate, often isolated and lonely metropolitan city center. After absorbing all of the life around me, I reflected upon the energy, joy, clarity, and healing that I felt permeating my inmost being from this place and these people.

It struck me as my son swayed to and fro on the swing set, kept in motion by my occasional push, that this gathering of culturally and ethnically diverse people, engaged in play with and enjoyment of each other and of the land and resources, was a perfect proleptic picture and paradigm of the new creation we read about in the book of Revelation, in which every nation, tribe, and tongue dwell together in the new earth, worshiping the Lamb and living in perfect harmony with God and one another. By *proleptic* I refer to the present inbreaking and experience of a reality that is complete only in the future. Only by living proleptically, that is, living now by the sure hope of the future, can we bring into the present the reign, rule, and transformative presence of the kingdom of God. A key component to the experience of the proleptic presence of the kingdom of God is the community of Christ engaged in transformative, cruciform worship that yields the presence of God's new-creation kingdom in the systems, structures, and individual lives of our communities and across the entire world.

As my time at the park was nearing an end, I noticed that while I was reflecting upon all of this dense theological stuff, a man dressed in traditional Jewish clothing and his son had come to use the swing directly next to Liam and me. The boy, a toddler around my son's age, began to laugh. Liam, upon hearing the laughter, looked at the boy and began laughing as well, reciprocating and participating in his new neighbor's joy. Both the boy's father and I smiled as we observed our sons in the midst of such simple contentment together. There was no hate, no violence, no co-ercion, and no pretend killing; there was only family, friendship, com-munity, participation, and joy. After a few minutes the boy's father ad-dressed me, "If only life could be as innocent and simple for us as it is for these guys now! If they only knew . . ." I responded by saying; "Yeah! I know, right?"

But inside of my mind and heart one thought and desire reverberated, albeit while remaining unspoken: *What if life really is meant to be that innocent and simple, but we've become so calloused, so confused, and so seduced and distracted by the narratives of this world that we've forgotten the simple truth of the one narrative that actually does matter, the gospel?*[2] *What if we remembered that the true story of what it means to be abun-dantly alive and human, the gospel, is not characterized by a retreat from, renunciation of, and graduation from simplicity, innocence, and ever-lasting peace, but rather it is driven by a power that seeks to retrieve and revive these things for the life of the world by the communal renovation of our hearts through the cruciformational worship of Jesus Christ?*

The kingdom of God is already here. Yet it is not fully present. The sin of the world still corrupts our experience of the proleptic inbreaking of the kingdom park of the new creation. However, the means to the pro-leptic presence of the new-creation park of the kingdom of God is not through walking in the way of passivity, acquiescence, or complacency in regard to the false narratives, rules, and patterns of this world. Rather, it is made present—enacted and received—through communal, worshipful walking in the way of the cross.

Through this cruciform existence as a worshiping community, the rec-onciled church becomes the means by which God reconciles the world to himself. When the reconciled become reconcilers, our communion with God and one another empowers us to refuse and contradict the world as it is and to see it transformed through the cruciform love of God—the one who created it and the one who is redeeming it.[3] The way to redemption is always through the communal worship and embodiment of the crucified God, through whom we receive the power to exit the narrative of this world and to rewrite life.

PART 2

CRUCIFORMATION

Worship in the Way of the Cross

3

AN INTRODUCTION TO
CRUCIFORMATION

(or, Toward a Theology of "Family Resemblance")

I'm not sure which is more disturbing to me: Victoria Osteen's quip about worship in which she said, "When you come to church, when you worship Him, you're not doing it for God really. You're doing it for yourself, because that's what makes God happy. Amen?"[1] or the oft-repeated phrase popular in evangelical churches about "performing worship for an audience of one" (referring to God as the sole audience member of a worship production that we create).[2] Both of these sayings trouble me. The first statement reveals a theology that essentially makes worship all about us while in the latter statement, worship is viewed in terms of a performance or production that we stage for the Almighty. Though I've never been in a church that openly espoused either view, I can certainly imagine what it might be like to participate in a worship team at a church in which worship is viewed as a self-indulgent and self-serving performance in which God is the sole audience member.

EXPERIENCE CHURCH:
WORSHIPING FOR GOD AND FOR OURSELVES

Imagine with me if you would: It is service number three of ten services on the Sunday before Christmas at Experience Church, a megachurch in Dallas consisting of five thousand members, complete with its own mini-shopping mall, a state-of-the-art food court and Noah's ark–themed bowling alley, a twentysomethings group called Rustic, a midthirties group called Rooted, a small group Bible study only open to people with mustaches, another small group for those who desire to have mustaches but do not yet have a mustache, a third mustache-related Bible study for people who greatly dislike mustaches but find themselves in relationships with people who have mustaches (this one includes a mustache counselor on site at each meeting for moral support whether for or against mustaches), an octogenarian fellowship group featuring fresh Jell-o and a weekly denture comparison and cleanliness committee, ExperienceKids (for 0-10 year olds), ExperienceTween (for 11-13 year olds), Experience-NewLife (for adolescent 14-18 year olds), ExperienceAdultolescence (for 19-year-old man-boys who live in their mothers' basements), and an assortment of worship bands consisting of one hundred total musicians, ninety-six of whom wear skinny jeans and scarves in July.

In addition, there are six men with flannel shirts who have very unkempt beards. One of them has a very pointy beard, and this is how you know that he's a true Calvinist. Pointy-beard guy is not like the other five non-pointy-bearded guys. Judging by their beards and by the fact that they've never read John Piper, it's probably safe to conclude that they are not really Reformed. Sure, they might have listened to some R. C. Sproul sermons and stuff, but they probably have never even heard of the *Institutes* or the Synod of Dort. And I bet they've never smoked a pipe or ranted at someone on social media about penal substitutionary atonement and supralapsarianism. Though all of these men have beards and wear flannel, none of the six are loggers. In fact, one of them (the guy with the pointy beard, of course) even claims to be allergic to wood. He often tells the tale of that fateful day during his childhood on which he received a horrible rash after building a treehouse in his backyard. Sadly, he could never again go in it. He just had to sit there and watch the treehouse remain beautifully unoccupied in the tree, all by itself, all through elementary school to middle school and on to high school. In fact, truth be told, that's why he grew a beard and became Reformed. It is also the case that to this day he has trouble finding adequate housing for himself because his only choices are between brick-based or fiberglass-based dwellings. These bearded men are the worship leaders.

The multiple flat-screen displays located on the walls, the stage, and on the back of each of the theater-style seats in the auditorium play a looped, prerecorded welcome message from Pastor Steve speaking to the congregation. Pastor Steve is a thirty-nine-year-old former linebacker with the New England Patriots turned evangelist and karate enthusiast. The video voice-over says, "We want to welcome you to Experience Church! We're so psyched that you've decided to 'do life' with us here. Sit back, relax, and get ready to experience God in worship because here at Experience Church the show is for you and for God." On the side of the screen a clock counts down the time until the start of the service: 5:00, 4:59, 4:58, 4:57 . . .

Attendees of the 10:00 a.m. showing of the ecclesial event are now mostly in their places, sipping their vanilla chai mocha latte cappuccino Frappuccinos. However, a few opted for bringing their own coffee as a protest against the fact that the coffee cups do not say "Merry Christmas."[3] Meanwhile, backstage Pastor Walt (one of the bearded worship pastors) is putting in his in-ear monitors and checking the levels. After combing his beard and putting on his scarf, Pastor Walt gathers the worship team and forms a circle for the preservice prayer.

"Lord," he begins, "we just want to thank you. We just want to lift up your name. We just want to give you all the praise because . . . you are God. Father God, we just want, Father God, to bring you the glory, Father God. We just want to glorify you, Father God, and worship you, Father God. Father God, you are the Father God, Father God. We just want to surrender, Lord, Father God. We want to play for you, Father God, as an audience, Father God, of one, Father God." During the prayer Winston, the charismatic drummer, shouts randomly as the prayer ramps up: "Yeeeees!" and "Thank ya, Lord!" and the quickly sputtered finale complete with hand movements, "Hal-le-lu-jah! Hal-le-lu-jah! Hal-le-lu-jah! Ha-lle-lu-jahhhhhhh! Father God." The bassist Ken is the token prayer-moaner of the group, letting out pseudosexual-sounding weird sighs of spiritual agreement sporadically during the prayer: "Mmmmm. Thank you, Lord" and "Ummmm-hmm!" with a staccato ending, followed by, "Yup. Hhhhhhhhallelujah. Mmmmm. Yes, Lord!" One other guy takes off his shoes during the prayer because he heard that Moses had done that once near some mountain a long time ago to be "spiritual and stuff." The other team members wish that he had left them on. After all, nothing spoils Christmas more than bare hairy hipster feet in close proximity to the nativity scene. The sanctimonious stench of pretension and feet is like the Christmas antigift that keeps on giving.

Meanwhile, Marie, the background vocalist, lays hands on Janine, the lead vocalist, and she has a word of knowledge for her: "The Lord is telling me right now that you're going to be a world-famous seafood chef with your own restaurant." Marie shudders, recalling both that she is severely allergic to oysters and also that she once received a minor but scary injury when she was bitten by one of the lobsters that her dad bought for the Fourth of July dinner. She had been trying to put it on a leash to take it for a walk. She had named it Montgomery. To this day, she doesn't know what is worse, the fact that the lobster didn't end up being her pet, or that she ended up subsequently eating him for lunch. And— here's the worst part and the locus of all the lobster-laden guilt— Montgomery was delicious! Oh, the shock! Oh, the guilt! Oh, the shame of pseudo-pet turned seafood-lunch deliciosity! Marie sometimes wakes up in the middle of the night screaming "Montgomery!" while simultaneously feeling equally drawn to both the aquarium and to the restaurant Red Lobster. One other member who was supposed to be on the team, Carl, wasn't able to make the worship event that day because his skinny jeans were still in the wash from the night before. He had spilled organic hummus on them at a Bohemian coffee shop that plays only music you've never heard of—after he had been to the Bogus Poets concert the previous night.[4] Carl just could not disrespect God Almighty by showing up to church in regular—or God forbid—baggy denim.

Granted, this is just a little far-fetched and hyperbolic, but you get the picture. Although I understand the desire to refer to worship as that which is performed for an audience of one, I think that it is potentially detrimental to our theology of worship and our practice of worship in and as the local church. God most certainly is not in need of our skilled musical performances in the way that this phrase suggests he would be, as if he is sitting around in heaven with a ticket to our worship show twiddling his thumbs and hoping, just hoping, that we'll play "In Christ Alone" again, and this time with a crescendo and a rousing modulation. Imagine God the Father, upon tuning in via Spirit satellite to your local congregation, shaking his head and turning to the seat on his right saying to Jesus, "Son, I'm so sorry that you have to sit through another butchering of '10,000 Reasons.' Why the guitarist is using a digital pedal instead of a $400 analog boutique delay pedal made by some obscure electronic music guru in his garage is beyond me. The resultant sound is so—shall I say—pedestrian and predictable."

Worship is not a performance that we put on for God, nor is it merely something that we do to make us existentially (and financially) happy, as it is for Osteen. Rather, in the act of worship we are transformed—through love enacted, received, sung, preached, and consumed in the sacraments—into the image of the God who is love. Through worship and the life of the community in Christ we are in the process of being fully renovated, redeemed, and reconciled so we might reflect the glory of God to one another and to the world. God desires worship not because it fulfills a need in him but because worship rightly orients us to him so that we might become like him. Worship is about our reorientation to a reality in which God is all in all, and in which we are in right relationship with him and with each other. This is worship that glorifies God. Insofar as worship is directed toward God, it is biblical worship, and insofar as that worship transforms us, it glorifies and magnifies God by renovating and sanctifying us. Thus worship is not a product that we create for God or for other human beings. It is instead a communal participation in the cruciform God, a very means by which we encounter Jesus in, with, and through the other in the context of the local church—for the sake of the reconciliation of all things and the redemption of the world through the church.

I refer to this entire process of communal conformity to the crucified God as cruciformation. By cruciformation I am playing on the word *cruciform* and the idea of spiritual formation by combining them into one word to suggest that spiritual formation, an integral and inseparable element of the gospel, is always an act of cruciformation—namely, formation in the way of the cross through the enactment and reception of the love of Jesus toward and from the other in community. In the remainder of this section of the book, we will look in depth at Paul's epistle to the Colossians. I propose this is one of the clearest places in the New Testament where the biblical pattern of and point of Christian worship and fellowship is explicated by the apostle.[5] Though we will be anchored in Colossians as our primary text, I will demonstrate how this underlying pattern of cruciformation through worship and communal ecclesial life is woven throughout the entire New Testament as a core truth of the efficacy and aim of the gospel of Jesus Christ, both for the life of the church and for the life of the world.

The basic thesis can be summed up like this: by embodying God's love through God's loving community, we become like the God who is love. Cruciformation involves a transformation of character through worship (embodying God's love) that takes place in a context (God's loving community, the church). The embodiment of love leads to an experiential knowledge that the apostle Paul calls "the knowledge of God." This knowledge is not the knowledge of facts and figures about a person. Rather, it is the experiential knowledge of a person—namely, Jesus Christ. When we know facts about a person, we can pass a history test about that person. But when we know a person, we have an experiential relationship with them. That experiential, relational knowledge causes us to begin to resemble them. In the case of cruciform worship, through embodying love, we begin to resemble the God who is love.

FAMILY RESEMBLANCE AND CRUCIFORMATION

When thinking through deep theological truths it is always helpful to have an illustration from real life to remind us of the key components of the particular theological argument. Theologian Michael Gorman has argued that the act of Jesus on the cross is an "act of family resemblance" with God the Father; Jesus acts in accord with who he is in his nature as a God of self-giving love.[6] In other words, on the cross Jesus doesn't behave in a manner that is out of character with who he is in his eternal glory. Rather, he reveals the greatness of his glory precisely and most profoundly through his humble, sacrificial death. The God who is eternal love as Father, Son, and Holy Spirit reveals his nature not through majestic detachment and divine distance but through cruciform involvement and incarnated immanence. The cross is not an exception to the rule of God's character; it is the norm, and that norm is love.

Just as Christ's sacrificial love on the cross resembles the nature of his Father as love, the family resemblances within our own families tell a story about who we are, how we became that way, and who we are becoming in and through our participation in our families. Thus in thinking through the varied elements that contribute to a theology of cruciformation, family and family resemblance can assist us in crystallizing abstract theological arguments into a tangible and approachable image to which we can continue to refer and return. Transformative worship involves character development (embodying God's love) through a context (the church) which leads to a cruciformation (transformation by, through, and for love). Likewise, in a family, our character is developed and formed in large part through participation in our particular context—namely, our family. Cruciformational worship functions through our active embodiment of the love of God in the loving community of Christ, the church. When we are engaged in this life of communal love, we become like the God who is love. Family life operates in a similar fashion regarding our formation. Through living according to the rules, expectations, and ethical/behavioral patterns of the family, we become certain types of people, for better or worse. We begin to resemble the people who belong to our family.[7]

In terms of our character, family resemblance requires a knowledge of the people we are coming to resemble. The kind of knowledge that transforms us, that causes us to resemble another human being, is not merely factual but relational and experiential. We arrive at this kind of knowledge by doing rather than by studying. I often encounter students who, when asked to explain why they act a certain way or believe a particular idea, respond, "It's all I've ever known." What they mean, of course, is that their life experience—and in large part, the influence of their family—has been set by the parameters that they experienced while growing up. When they come into my undergraduate classes, many of them are just beginning to realize that the rest of their life is now a response to these initial experiences and familial boundaries.

The response to the result of these newly illuminated family resemblances, these ingrained ideals and unconscious habits, can be varied. Upon becoming aware of one's resemblances—the character traits and beliefs that arise from the context and practices of our upbringing—we can affirm, reject, abandon, protect, critique, reform, or ignore them.

Experiential knowledge within the family leads to the formation of character and family resemblance. But how? What does that look like in real life? How does personal, experiential knowledge transform us? I'll share a few examples from the context of my own family life to show how real, experiential knowledge requires sacrifice and how familial sacrifice shapes us even as we shape others through it. In giving these examples, it will be obvious that I am not holding out my own family as some sort of pristine model for Christian living. Rather, I'm speaking from my own experience, which is all I have. I invite you, as you read, to think of examples from your own experiences with your families that correspond to this theme of family resemblance.

There is a notable difference between knowing facts about my son Liam and having the kind of understanding that comes from experiencing the ups and downs of his life firsthand as his father. His birth date, his middle name, his place of birth, hair color, and eye color are facts about my son articulated on his birth certificate. If someone read that certificate and determined that they know facts about Liam, they'd technically be correct. If on the basis of these basic facts, however, someone claimed to actually know my son as a fellow human being, that claim would be universally rejected. Knowing about someone doesn't constitute an experiential, personal kind of knowledge. On the other hand, as Liam's dad, my experiential knowledge of my son and his experience of me consist of our experiences as members of the same family. Sure, I can rattle off some basic facts about him, but I can also speak at length and in great detail about his adorable idiosyncrasies, which I know firsthand from being his father.

I can recall our conversation over breakfast this past March. He revealed his latest dream—a little mischievous mouse who stole my car and a ghost who was on his bedroom wall. As I type this, I am staring directly at a Barber Direct Drive guitar distortion pedal sitting on my bookshelf in my office. This piece of musical equipment survived (and works great!) after Liam threw it into the toilet, where it bathed for several minutes before my wife ultimately discovered and rescued it. On June 24, 2016, I posted the following on social media: "Less than a year after its release, I can say with certainty that the movie *Zootopia* stands the test of time. . . . And by that I mean it stands the test of being viewed forty-seven times in a row within a two-week period, whilst still retaining its awesomeness." It is one thing to read that post and be amused by the fact that my toddler son is delighted by watching the same movie over and over again ad infinitum. It is an entirely a different kind of knowing, however, to actually sit through the forty-seven viewings of the movie with him. Being there and being invested make the difference.

The kind of deep, experiential knowledge that I am emphasizing is what builds character. In the context of the church, this is a knowledge obtained by being there with the other. It is a knowledge derived from a community of interpersonal interaction through which we experience Christ in the other and the other experiences Christ through us. In the church, knowledge of Christ is not merely the acquisition of theological facts about Christ; it is the knowledge of Christ himself experienced through one another.

The same kind of experiential knowledge holds true for other members of my family, and in ways that go beyond the idiosyncratic, fun elements of toddler illogic. Caring for a newborn infant who has colic, for example, requires a commitment to ceaselessly comforting a child who is, by definition, inconsolable. No one who has actually dealt with a colicky baby (as we did with Liam) would really resonate with someone who hasn't gone through it but has read about it on Wikipedia, noting that "it sounds pretty rough!" Of course it is rough, and one could in some sense empathize with the parents of a colicky baby without experiencing it for themselves. Yet the knowledge that comes through cosuffering with your child in their discomfort—of resolving to care for the child for however long it takes, of charging through the daily tasks that follow even without any sleep—is a much deeper, more experiential form of knowing than what is obtained through anything less than being there in the midst of life with another person. Caring for a colicky baby forms the child through sacrificial love and forms the caring parent through the perseverance of suffering love.

There is a massive difference—we would all agree—between simply knowing about someone's suffering and living with them in the midst of their suffering for weeks, months, years, and even decades. Whether the person is a child, spouse, parent, or grandparent, it is incredibly hard and heartbreaking to be present with a loved one in the midst of their suffering. However, most of us also intuitively understand that true love is itself a co-suffering love. It is a love that exercises a long obedience in the same direction and thereby builds up both the sufferer and the cosufferer through its power and perseverance.[8] It is a love that, like the love of Jesus Christ, transforms us from the context of a community, a family of believers.

CONCLUSION: TOWARD A THEOLOGY OF FAMILY RESEMBLANCE

Without being too simplistic, most would say that the governing attitudes and behaviors of a family significantly contribute to the nature of that family's character. Thus for a family characterized by anger, hostility, and violence, family resemblance becomes something to escape rather than something to perpetuate. Many of us have, to varying extents, experienced the effects of a broken home. None of us lives in a utopian, holy household. Many of us have also been blessed, however, to have some family members who demonstrated the sacrificial love of Christ to us. Through our knowledge of those family members, we have been changed through love to become agents of love in our own families. Our delight consists in cherishing our resemblance to those family members who first loved us and whose loving disposition is now carried on through us as we embody and perpetuate the powerful presence and practice of sacrificial love in our own homes, families, and communities.

So it is too for cruciformation through and as the church. As we enact and receive the love of God as his people, we become God's community of love, the church. And through this community we experience a transformational renewal—a cruciformation—into the image of the God who is love, Jesus Christ.

CRUCIFORM KNOWLEDGE

Encountering Christ Through Cruciform Worship

C hristlike character formation through the church community leads to cruciformation. We must keep this sequence in mind as we go deeper into a theology of the cruciformation that happens when we worship by walking in the way of the cross. This is how the family resemblance among God the Father, God the Son, and God the Holy Spirit becomes a reality for us, his adopted sons and daughters. The embodiment of God's love allows us to be conformed to Christ in his loving community, the church. Through this process of enacting and receiving love, we become like the God who is love. But how does this occur? Cruciformation is rooted in the reception of knowledge of Christ that comes by walking in the way of God and worshiping with the people of God. Thereby we are renewed in the image of God. The cruciformation of the church takes place through the cruciform presence of Christ, whom we encounter in one another as a worshiping community.

KNOWLEDGE THROUGH ACTIVITY:
BEDTIME RITUALS AND FAMILY RESEMBLANCE

At the heart of this chapter is the idea that a good deal of what we know, we arrive at through our actions and our experiences. In particular, we gain knowledge of the people in our lives primarily through our personal interactions and experiences with them in the context of our daily lives. The idea was put forth in the last chapter that our cruciformation in, through, and as the church involves a kind of positive formation into a resemblance with the family disposition of divine love. Through belonging to Christ's family we begin to resemble Christ's character by embodying the others-centered, self-giving love of the cross. The main point of this chapter is to biblically and theologically articulate that this formation through the knowledge of Christ is—through and through—one derived from the Spirit-empowered actions of the believer in community.

This process of transformation through action is not unique to the church. Rather, it is typical of how virtue and character are formed in human beings in general. Take, for example, my son Liam's bedtime ritual. Every evening when bedtime is upon us, the ritual begins in much the same way. First, we have to indicate to him that he cannot watch anymore television because it is time for bed. Depending on the evening either this provokes a dramatic ordeal in which he attempts to convince us that we should let him continue watching TV, or he simply complies and begins step two, the selection of the books. Without fail, each night Liam picks three books to read and we sit together as a family to read them. Currently, he is really into the book *If You Give a Mouse a Cookie*, and that book is basically selected every night. A close second is a beautifully illustrated book titled *Good Night, God Bless*, which Liam refers to as "Boy Hachoo" because he thinks "God Bless" is a reference to sneezing. Inevitably, we finish whichever of the three books he has selected and then he tries to squeeze a "surprise" fourth book into the mix by saying, "Lassssssssst boooook?" So sometimes we'll read a fourth, because (as Liam knows) I am totally easy to manipulate.

After the books Liam brushes his teeth. He can almost reach the bathroom sink, but he still needs a bit of a boost. So he requests to stand on "pee pee chair" which is a small potty that converts into a stepping stool. Sometimes said chair is not in the bathroom. When this is the case, a quest for the pee pee chair ensues along with a ceaseless chorus of questioning, "Where's pee pee chair? Where's pee pee chair, Daddy?" Once located, we bring it into the bathroom, Liam jumps on and grabs his toothbrush, and I help him brush his teeth.[1]

Midway through the brushing, Liam always opens the middle door of the cupboard, to which I yell "Don't!"

To this, he responds in a surprised manner, "Hey, shampoo!" when he sees in the cupboard a bottle of special edition Minions shampoo that we never use.

Last, we go into the bedroom where the tucking in ritual commences. Initially, I tuck him in, and then I turn on the light that projects blue stars onto the ceiling. Then I give him a hug and a kiss, and I go to get my wife. I leave while she completes the tuck-in time, and then about three minutes later I will hear her call, "Daddy, Liam wants you to come back in." Then, I return briefly, he pretends to steal my nose, and we say good night.

From my telling of this story, it is evident that my knowledge of my son's bedtime ritual is exhaustive and experiential. Pertinent to this chapter's main emphasis, a new game has emerged during the daytime in which I pretend that I am Liam and my son pretends to be me. It is so amusing to me that during this playtime game he acts exactly the same as I do when I tuck him in. He tucks me into his tiny toddler bed. He puts the covers on me, he puts the star light on, and he says good night and "I love you." He then goes to get my wife to make her say good night to me. It is quite detailed, actually.

Liam's embodiment and enacting of my nighttime rituals exhibit the gentle, caring attitude he has observed and encountered in our own care of him. His acquaintance with and knowledge of this disposition comes from his direct experience of my wife and me, from our actions over the course of life lived together as a family. Liam's response in the game indicates to me that his knowledge of us causes him—in some real and significant sense—to resemble us in his actions, behaviors, and character. Likewise, it is this kind of a lived experience that causes the church to be conformed to the love of God through the experiential knowledge that comes through walking in his ways, according to his will.

KNOWLEDGE OF GOD THROUGH
WALKING IN THE WAY OF GOD

A common mistake when theologizing about the topic of worship is to define the word in a manner that suggests it refers solely to the musical portion of a weekly worship service. We often refer to "the worship" as the set of songs at the beginning or at the end of the service. A pastor might instruct his ministerial team about the forthcoming service as follows: "We'll have an opening prayer, and then some worship [i.e., music], and then we'll continue the service with a sermon and an offering, and then we'll do some more worship to conclude." I will spend a significant amount of time specifically addressing the role of musical worship in later chapters. In particular, I will unpack Colossians 3:16 which states: "Let the word of Christ abundantly make a home among you with all wisdom by means of teaching and admonishing one another, through psalms, hymns, and spiritual songs, by means of singing them with your hearts to God through the grace of reciprocity" (my translation; see also Eph 5:19).

It is rarely noted that the force of the Greek behind the words "psalms, hymns, and spiritual songs" and the participle "singing" indicate that these activities are the means by which the transformative word about Christ dwells in the believers. We often assume that the indwelling of the Word and the admonishing and the teaching ministries refer only or primarily to the ministry of preaching. While it is, of course, true that preaching is regarded by the New Testament to be one avenue of the ministry of the Word, in Colossians we encounter a different emphasis and medium for the indwelling Word of God: musical worship! It is important to note, however, that I do not intend to refer to music alone when using the word *worship*. Such an oversimplification misunderstands and misrepresents the biblically revealed, multifaceted nature and expressions of worship that are demonstrated, for example, in Colossians. Thus it is more biblically sound to speak broadly of worship as the communal life, customs, culture, and practices of the people of God, the church, through which God is honored and his people are transformed. These are the new-creation antidotes to many of the defining practices and values that we observed in the fallen-creation park such as selfishness, self-centeredness, and the myth of redemptive violence.

Let us begin by considering the inner logic of cruciformation, starting with Colossians 1:9-10. Here we come into contact with the essential features of a New Testament theology of worship in the way of the cross.

And so, we have not ceased praying for you, from the day we first heard about you, asking that you may be filled with the knowledge of his will by means of all spiritual wisdom and (spiritual) understanding in order to walk in a manner worthy of the Lord, in all scrupulous attentiveness, with the result that you bear fruit by means of every good work, and with the result that you grow in the knowledge of God. (Col 1:9-10, my translation)[2]

The basic summary of the verses' teaching is that through communally discovering God's will, we as the church are able to walk in accord with God's will. And this results in two realities: (1) the bearing of the fruit of good works and (2) the knowledge of God. We must ask, why should this be considered a specifically communal and ecclesial walking out of the faith? Paul's exhortations here really have nothing to do with the church, or worship, but rather are charging individual Christians (who may or may not be connected to the church) to engage in Christlike behavior. I find the latter interpretation uncompelling for several reasons.

First, though it is impossible to detect in the English translation, all of the references in this passage to "you" are, in fact, plural in the original Greek. Thus when Paul writes "we have not ceased praying for you," this should be read as "ya'll," or "you all"—that is, as a reference to the entire, plural group of the church as a whole and not merely as a communicatory gesture to individuals (then or now). Second, all of the verbal forms in these verses are plural, thus indicating that being filled with the knowledge of God's will, bearing of fruit of good works, and growing in the knowledge of God are all activities and realities that are communally enacted and communally achieved. Third, the epistle itself is most certainly not directed to an individual or to a group of individual free agents—whether individuals in Colossae or autonomous individuals in contemporary times. Rather, the epistle is expressly addressed to a plural entity—namely, the church, or as Paul puts it, "the saints and faithful brothers in Christ at Colossae" (Col 1:2).

If we can momentarily fast-forward to the aim of Paul's argument in Colossians as a whole, we will gain a helpful perspective as to the general overarching trajectory of his teaching of cruciformational worship and

communal life in the epistle. Paul argues that the believer is perfected by
the knowledge of God obtained by walking in God's ways in a life of communal worship and fellowship (Col 1:9-10; 18). Furthermore, this perfection takes place through a renewal for which the knowledge of God is
the primary means (Col 3:9-11). The renewal, Paul maintains, is achieved
through the communal enactment and reception of divine love in the
church, which acts as a mechanism of transformative, binding unity (Col
3:12-14). Last (and surprisingly!), this process is partially achieved
through the indwelling peace and word of Christ made present to the
church in psalms, hymns, and spiritual songs (Col 3:15-16). Thus musical
worship, we will see, plays a central role in the process of cruciformation.

GOD'S WILL DIRECTS OUR WALKING,
WHICH LEADS TO KNOWLEDGE

In Colossians 1:9-10 we notice instantly that Paul's prayer begins with a
petition that "the knowledge of [God's] will" would be made available to
the church. This is not the kind of pop Christianity pursuit of God's will
that seeks to discover whether one should become a dentist, police of-
ficer, professor, etc. Rather, Paul prays that the community might know
the will of God so the believers might walk in accord with that will. The
knowledge of God's will, therefore, serves a particularly moral and
ethical purpose instead of functioning like a form of Christian fortune-
telling or vocation mysticism.

In other words, God's will (at least here) really is about God, about his
character and how he wants us to live in light of that as people created
in his image. It is easy to pass over the significance of seemingly incidental words in the original Greek and in the English translations. The
phrase "so as to walk" (ESV) and in my own translation "in order to walk"
are renderings of the Greek grammatical structure that introduces what
is called a purpose clause. The takeaway here (as we move on in the argument) is that the prayer for the knowledge of God's will in the church
is expressly and specifically invoked to inform a communal walking in
accord with that will. This communal walking leads to two realties, according to Paul: namely, (1) the bearing of fruit by means of good works,
and (2) the knowledge of God.

SANCTIFICATION THROUGH COOPERATIVE CRUCIFORMITY

The fact that human agency in worship and life is meant to contribute spiritually to the salvation and transformation of individuals is quite disturbing to many Protestants who wrongly conflate the doctrine of justification by faith with the term *gospel*. In this understanding, any discussion of works at all reeks of works-righteousness, defined in Lutheran terms as those human religious works and good deeds done based on the erroneous presumption that God will save individuals on the basis of their own merit.[3] Many Protestant and evangelical theologies assess in a totally negative way any grace-empowered, Spirit-driven human participation in the process of sanctification—that is, the process of becoming holy as God is holy. The gospel certainly includes the doctrine of justification. It should not, however, be totally equated with it. The gospel includes a host of metaphors and realities related to the justification, sanctification, transformation, and renovation of the character of believers.

The mystery of the Christian life is that through pouring oneself out for the sake of the other, we find ourselves paradoxically built up through love rather than exhausted by it. We become more human by loving like God loves, and we become like God through love, because God is love, and he himself defines what it means to live lovingly through the sacrifice of Jesus Christ. Therefore, Christianity is not just a religion about how to get saved or be justified but it is also a way of life that transforms us into the image of God in Christ Jesus. This is, in fact, the entire point of cruciformation! The tendency, therefore, to recoil at the idea of moral transformation as being located within the gospel—that is, within the project of the redemption and the salvation of individuals and the church—must be tempered and corrected by the New Testament and the teachings of Jesus himself (e.g., Mt 5–7 and Jn 15).

The important thing not to miss here is that through the mechanisms of communal, active, Spirit-governed walking and ethical living in the church, transformation (i.e., fruit bearing and good works) and revelation (i.e., the knowledge of God) occur. It follows that without the believers' cooperation with the spiritually given will of God toward a transformational and revelatory ethical life and encounter with God, believers will be at a spiritual detriment in regard to their salvation. This is not to say they will not ultimately be saved, but it is to say that the worshiping community does not exist to be merely declared righteous and to remain as sinful wretches, incapable of growth in Christ.

Although it is not evident in the English translations, the Greek adverbial participle translated as "growing" (ESV "increasing") is a participle of result, indicating the result of our walk, the knowledge of God. Just like my son arrived at his knowledge of bedtime rituals by experiencing them through personal activity and interaction, so too the knowledge of Christ comes through actively walking in accord with his will and his ways, and embodying his cruciform character. Thus—to return to our theme of the function of Spirit-inspired works and activity in the Christian life—in this verse, Paul communicates to us that the Spirit-empowered, transformative, cooperative, communal human activity in the worshiping church results in a growth in the knowledge of God.[4] However, one must ask: What is meant by the "knowledge of God," and why is it important to Christian sanctification and growth?

KNOWLEDGE OF GOD AS KNOWLEDGE OF "WHO GOD IS IN HIMSELF"

Many readers assume, based on an overly cognitive understanding of faith, that what Paul is referring to here is a growth in doctrinal formulations and theological acumen. When we hear "knowledge of God"— especially in evangelical circles—we tend to think primarily about Bible studies, theological degrees and courses, statements of faith, and other information-based phenomena related to the quest for the accumulation of facts about God. It is assumed that one's level of spiritual maturity, spiritual health, and spiritual growth is somehow contingent upon and directly correlated with the adequate acquisition of correct theological ideas. This conception of a one-to-one correspondence between theological learnedness and holiness must be unequivocally rejected. While I in no way want to suggest that doctrine is not important—it most assuredly is—such an intellectualized understanding of sanctification fails experientially, exegetically, and theologically.[5]

Experientially, it is by no means evident to me that the people with the highest academic training and advanced degrees in the Bible and theology are by default the most spiritually healthy or spiritually advanced. On the contrary, more often than not, Christian academics are among those most at risk of falling victim to spiritual fatigue and for contracting the spiritually emaciating disease of pride. The idea that knowledge of God should be viewed primarily as a knowledge of theological facts and systems about God is unsustainable. While the Bible certainly does speak about the knowledge of doctrine as one way of knowing, a more common meaning of *knowledge* refers to the experiential knowledge of encounter— that is to say, the intimate knowledge of a person rather than the abstract knowledge of a series of propositional statements about a person.[6]

Theologically, a theory of knowledge that is essentially cognitive and intellectualist excludes in advance children, people with developmental disabilities, and folks who are simply unintentionally ignorant of theological jargon pertaining to the doctrine of God. In the "knowledge equals correct theological facts" interpretation of the knowledge of God, all of these groups of people (and more) are barred from being included among those considered to be spiritually growing and spiritually healthy members of the kingdom in any real sense. After all, if the litmus test of the kingdom for spiritual health is the ability to wax eloquent about the concept of perichoresis in the Trinity and the consubtantiality of the Godhead, then my son is in big trouble—and, really, so are most adults, including theologians! As a Christian theologian I would think it totally bogus if, upon pulling up to the pearly gates whilst doing a wheelie on my heavenly Harley-Davidson, I was given a Scantron bubble answer sheet for an SAT-style theological knowledge exam which served as the official Spiritual Health Assessment of Heaven.

This "knowledge as facts" view, furthermore, makes little sense compared to Paul's use of the concept of knowledge elsewhere, such as in 1 Corinthians 13:9, 12 in which he states: "For we know in part and we prophesy in part. . . . For now we see in a mirror dimly, but then face to face. Now I know in part; then I shall know fully, even as I have been fully known." This metaphor demands a view of knowledge that is personal, relational, and experiential rather than propositional and doctrinal. Otherwise we would have to believe that what Paul knows and sees dimly in a mirror is a rather fuzzy looking list of propositions about a person, rather than an image of the person himself. Likewise, when Jesus in Matthew 7:21-23 tells the false disciples who had said "Lord, Lord" to him "depart from me, I never knew you," he is clearly not saying "I never knew a series of propositional facts about you such as whether you enjoy oysters, country music, reruns of *Mr. Ed*, and cotton candy flavored chewing gum!" Rather, Jesus is indicating that he never had a personal, experiential, intimate knowledge of them despite their use of the Hebrew form of double naming which expresses such a relationship.[7] We all know basic facts about potentially hundreds, or even thousands, of individuals through Internet social media sites, but how many of these individuals do we actually know, encounter, and experience as people? Most people recognize intuitively that knowledge of a person is so much more than the sum total of a list of facts about that person. Yet theologically, we often behave in the opposite fashion. We act as though a list of ideas about Jesus constitutes knowledge of him, and this couldn't be further from the truth.

James K. A. Smith sums up this idea helpfully, situating it within a discussion of the communal formation that takes place through worship. He writes:

> Being a disciple of Jesus is not primarily a matter of getting the right ideas and doctrines and beliefs into your head in order to guarantee proper behavior; rather, it's a matter of being the kind of person who loves rightly—who loves God and neighbor and is oriented to the world by the primacy of that love. We are made to be such people by our immersion in the material practices of Christian worship—through affective impact, over time, of sights and smell in water and wine.[8]

In Colossians, knowledge is not functioning primarily as a reference to knowledge about God, it is knowledge of God himself. As we observed, the knowledge of God's will leads to the walking, which results in the works, which act as a witness to the character and being of God himself. Thus the knowledge of God is not a primarily doctrinal knowledge, or even a general knowledge of God's existence. It is rather a knowledge of the character of God—that is, a knowledge of who God is in himself, which is precisely derived from enacting the purposes of his will, which likewise testifies to God's own character. Later in the epistle, in Colossians 3:10, we discover the ultimate aim of this relational, experiential knowledge of God. Paul tells us there that believers are being renewed in knowledge according to the image of the one who created them—namely, Christ. In light of what we find implicit in Colossians 1:9-10, we can conclude that in Colossians 3:10, the means by which the renewal in knowledge into the image of the divine Christ takes place is precisely a communal process of receiving, enacting, and walking in the will of God, in the context and through the instrument of the worshiping community, the church.[9]

We can go even further by saying that through worshipful walking in and as the church we come into an encounter, not merely with who God is in himself in some general sense, but specifically with the knowledge of who God is in Christ. After all, Paul proclaims and teaches Christ to lead believers into perfection (Col 1:28).[10] Likewise, in Colossians 2:2, Paul overtly states that "the knowledge of God's mystery" is, in fact, Christ himself. Following the same trajectory, Paul returns to this theme in Colossians 2:3 in which "all the treasures of wisdom and knowledge" are said to be hidden "in Christ." Finally, in Colossians 3:10, we discover the entire point of this knowledge-encounter of Christ—namely, our renewal "in knowledge" according to the image of the creator, who is clearly Christ. Therefore, the theme of knowledge in Colossians is intimately linked with an experiential, personal knowledge and encounter of the living Christ arrived at through the communal enactment and reception of God's will and character in worship. Since all the fullness of deity is said to dwell bodily in Christ (Col 2:9) who is the image of the invisible God (Col 1:15), we can conclude that the knowledge of God himself is, in some sense, knowledge of Christ as God, and that this knowledge comes through our life together as a worshiping community.

CONCLUSION: CRUCIFORM KNOWLEDGE

Recalling the initial thesis of this chapter—namely, that by walking in the way of God and worshiping with the people of God we are renewed in the image of God—some progress has been made toward uncovering the inner logic of Paul's cruciformational view of the worshiping church. The knowledge of who God is in himself that results from communally walking according to the will of God forms us and is made present by us to the other (and to us through the other) by the power of the Holy Spirit in the church. The content of this knowledge is Jesus Christ himself, the context is Christ's loving community, the church, and the result is the cruciformation of the people of God. Just as Liam became acquainted with the bedtime rituals of care and gentleness in our household through having firsthand experiential knowledge of them, enough that he could act them out himself during playtime, so too the church is being formed into a family resemblance of love, through love, as part of the family of the God who is love. We shall now observe how this knowledge perfects us through and for cruciform love.

5

CRUCIFORM PERFECTION

Completion in Christ Through Cruciform Community

M oral and ethical transformation into Christlikeness necessarily occurs in the context of a community. The church, for Paul, is not an optional addendum to a personal quest toward Christlike perfection. Rather, it is the location of and means by which those who have received the wisdom of God and the will of God through the Spirit encounter the love of Christ himself through the other and are thereby transformed into the image of his love. This is the heart and center of the life of the church as a worshiping community. The life and worship of the church exists to bring God glory by making us like the glorious God. The fact that this perfection takes place "in Christ" (Col 1:28) functions to identify the sphere or location of the perfecting activity.[1] Additionally, the phrase "in Christ" serves to emphasize the agency of Christ as the one who makes us perfect. These two ideas (location and agency) are not mutually exclusive, and in fact, both senses of the phrase are operative in the context of Colossians.

For Paul, this perfection, this renewal in knowledge according to the image of Christ—this putting on of the new humanity that is in accord with Christ, this moral, salvific, and ethical aim of his—happens in and through a people, a people in whom Christ is all and in all. Christ is in all precisely through communal, cruciform participation in the people of

God, the new humanity. Those who are "in Christ" undergo a communal, Christlike transformation—a cruciformation. Love itself is the defining characteristic of God and Christ, and the bond that leads to perfection. We are renewed in knowledge not by some filling that happens while we stand by passively but by the God-enabled will, wisdom, and works rooted in the exercise of worship and communal love that defines the character of God himself. The self-giving love of Christ himself, of course, most clearly exemplifies this love. Thus we become like God by participating in his love through enactment and reception in the place where Christ is all and in all—namely, the church.

COMMUNAL PARTICIPATION IN THE KNOWLEDGE OF GOD LEADS TO OUR PERFECTION IN CHRIST

Considering that the knowledge of who God is in Christ is not a statement of faith or a list of theological ideas but is, in fact, an encounter with and an embodying and incarnating of a person, then we must then ask this: What are the further benefits and effects of this encounter with the living God through the worshiping community of the church?

It is clear from an exegesis of Colossians 1:28 that Paul's goal in "warning and teaching" is to present "every person perfect in Christ." In Colossians 3:14, Paul precisely defines this perfection as resulting from love both of the Christian in the context of the church and from the church toward the world. Furthermore, we can say with certainty that this perfection, accomplished (according to Col 1:28) in and through Christ, according to Colossians 3:10, results from a renewal in knowledge of Christ the Creator.[2] In Colossians 3:14, Paul describes love as a perfecting bond that exists between the members of the new humanity in Christ—that is, the church. It is the virtue that governs all other Christian relationships. Therefore, in sum, the aim of our fellowship is to experience perfection in and by Christ, and this is accomplished in and by Christ, meaning "in and through church."[3] This perfection takes place through love which is itself—for Colossians—modeled after the self-giving love of Jesus Christ, the ultimate revelation of the cruciform character of God in whose knowledge we are being renewed precisely through the enactment and reception of this love in the context of the church.

This theme of Christian sanctification through the communal life and worship of the church is not limited to Colossians. It appears with a high degree of frequency throughout the New Testament. A clear parallel to this pattern of cruciformation occurs in 1 John 2:5, where the author indicates that whoever keeps God's word will experience the love of God being perfected in him. Likewise, in 1 John 4:7, love for one another indicates that one has been "born of God" and that one "knows God." Thus for John, the enactment of cruciform, divine love in the community of Christ is the evidence that one has encountered God. This makes all the more sense when we observe that in the very next verse John explicitly states that "God is love" (1 Jn 4:8, cf. 1 Jn 4:16).

Therefore, in the writings of John, much like in the writings of Paul, the knowledge of God's Word (for Paul in Colossians it is God's will) leads to an active living out of that Word in the community of God. This thereby leads to the believers' perfection in and through living out love in communal reciprocity. Relatedly, for both John and Paul this active ecclesial, communal life—marked by the engagement of love toward the other, the reception of love from the other, and the embodiment of love for the sake of the world—witnesses to the knowledge of the God who is himself defined as love. We become like the God who is love through loving in the community of God's love. Christlike character is built through belonging to and living lovingly in the church community. This ultimately issues forth in a cruciformation of both the individual and the church.

The writings of James also contain this pattern of a trajectory toward perfection and completion in Christ through faith that is alive in love. James 1:3-4 presents an observable sequence: faith, when tested, leads to steadfastness, and steadfastness leads to perfection. Further, in James 2:22, the apostle reveals that faith itself is perfected by works, a theme that coheres very well with Paul's arguments in Colossians and is parallel to what Paul says in Galatians 5:6—true faith is active, working, and energized through love.[4]

We also find the theme of perfection in Christ to be a central concept throughout the Pauline corpus beyond what we have already articulated in the epistle to the Colossians. First Corinthians 13:10, for example, speaks of "the perfect" coming when "the partial" has passed away. In the context of 1 Corinthians 13 this is tied to the theme of an increase in knowledge. Pertinent to the theme of cruciformity in Paul is the statement that Paul makes about perfection in 2 Corinthians 12:9. There, the power of God in the Christian is "made perfect by weakness."

Thus for Paul, the power and grace of God for the believer operates in a cruciform way. Believers experience the perfecting power of the cross not by an escape from suffering but precisely through it. In this abiding in Christ by cruciform suffering, the love of God is perfected in us because the love of God itself is a suffering love.[5]

PERFECTION THROUGH PUTTING ON THE COMMUNAL CHRIST

While all of this may seem interesting in a conversation about the church and the necessity of community, you might be asking what this really has to do with worship. Keeping in mind that we have already defined worship as far more than the presermon musical portion of a Sunday gathering, rather favoring a broader conception of worship as the ecclesiologically rooted patterns of life, liturgy, culture, and community that shape us into the image of God, we can in one sense consider everything presented thus far as a discussion of worship and its effect on the believers in the church. We have essentially been looking closely at the inner logic of how Paul and the authors of the New Testament conceived of worship and communal life as an agent of the transformation of communities, individuals, and the world. Believers walk in the way of God and worship with the people of God, and thereby, they are renewed in the image of God. This is how cruciformation occurs. Our character is transformed by love, through love, and for love in the community of love, the church.

All of this, then, is integral to the underlying "why" and "how" of Christian worship. Worship leaders and people involved in worship arts roles in the church will find Colossians 3:9-17 to be particularly illuminating. In these verses the themes of knowledge, community, perfection, and love all come together in the context of the church at worship. Paul writes (and notice our key themes thus far in italics below):

Do not lie to one another (2nd person pl.), because you (pl.) have taken off the old man (sg.) and his practices and you have put on the 'new, being-*renewed-in-knowledge*-according-to-the-image-of-its-creator' human (sg.)[6] Here there is not Greek or Jew, circumcision or uncircumcision, barbarian, Scythian, slave, free, but Christ is all and in all. Therefore, put on (pl.), as elect ones of God, holy and beloved, gut-wrenching compassion, kindness (sg.), humility (sg.), meekness (sg.), and patience (sg.). Put these on in the manner of bearing with (pl.) one another, in the manner of forgiving (pl.) each other. If one of you has a complaint against another one of you as also the Lord has forgiven you (pl.), in this manner also you (pl.) forgive them. And governing all of these things is *love, which is the communal bond (sg.) which leads to perfection.* And let the peace of Christ rule in your hearts for which purpose also you have been called into one body, and be thankful. *Let the word about Christ abundantly make a home among you with all wisdom by means of teaching and admonishing one another, through psalms, hymns and spiritual songs, by means of singing them with your hearts to God through the grace of reciprocity.* And whatever you do, in word or in deed, do all things in the name of the Lord Jesus, giving thanks to God the Father through him. (Col 3:9-17, my translation)

This segment of verses can be summed up in the following way: through taking off the old way of being human represented by Adam (lit. "the Old Man"), and putting on the new way of being human—namely, Jesus himself—we are involved in a renewal in the image of God that takes place through communal knowledge of Jesus and leads to the perfection of character for believers and the church. Paul explains just how this knowledge of Jesus is made manifest in the local church: (1) putting on Jesus as a collective body, the church; (2) enacting and receiving the cruciform love, humility, forgiveness, and character of Jesus through the other in the context of the church, which acts as a perfecting bond of unity; and finally, (3) singing psalms, hymns, and spiritual songs through which Christ "makes a home" among (Col 3: 16). Thus once again in this culminating verse, Paul contributes to a New Testament cruciformational theology of ecclesial life and worship by linking the church to renewal in the knowledge of God. This renewal takes place through walking together in God's will, according to his Word, by which we encounter and are renewed by God himself in Christ. By walking in love, and worshiping in love, we become like the God who is love, Jesus Christ.

You (Pl.) not You (Sg.): The Communally Clothed, Corporate Christ

The first thing to note is that in this passage—as has been Paul's custom thus far—all verbs and references to "you" are plural. Thus the addressees here are not conceived of as a collection of individual free agents randomly assembled in the same location but rather as one united, inseparable entity. This unity is further expressed when Paul grounds the command to avoid lying in the fact that they, as a plural entity, have taken off a singular reality, "the old man" (Col 3:9 my translation). Some translations render the Greek phrase as "the old self" thus turning it into a statement that expresses the fact that each individual believer has taken off a former existential reality and identity.[7] This reading, however, is quite problematic. It turns what is grammatically a collective singular concept—namely, "the old man" (or "old humanity," "old way of being human")—and replaces it with a concept that is merely individualistic rather than corporate. Paul's entire point, though, is that individual people have taken off a former, shared, sinful, corporate way of living characterized by Adam, the representative of the old humanity.

The clothing metaphor continues by noting that those who have taken off the old man have put on the new man, Jesus Christ. Once again, a plural group puts on a singular object, the body of Christ. Therefore, what we have here is not in the first place a reference to the existential "old selves" of individuals being taken off, but a former way of being human in which these Christians previously shared. Paul describes this old humanity earlier as "things that are on earth," which are to be put to death (Col 3:2, 5), on account of which the wrath of God is coming (Col 3:6), and which corresponds to the former lives (walking) of the Christians (Col 3:7). This interpretation of Colossians 3:9-10—in which a corporate way of life represented by corporate solidarity with, and incorporation into, an individual (whether Adam or Christ)—makes the best sense of the initial plural exhortations followed by a singular concept.[8]

PAUL AS EXEMPLAR OF CRUCIFORM SUFFERING

This concept of believers' incorporation and participation in Christ—into which they enter a corporate, transformative body—is central both to the epistle to the Colossians and to the entire New Testament. Earlier in Colossians, Paul states that he wants the Colossians, "those at Laodicea," and all who have not seen him face to face to know about his great struggles on their behalf, that their hearts might be encouraged (Col 2:1-2). Why, though, would Paul's suffering bring the church encouragement? Wouldn't it more likely discourage the people in these churches?

Paul answers that question in the second part of Colossians 2:2. He notes that this knowledge of his suffering for them would result in their being knit together by love. The sense that Paul intends here is one in which the hearts of the Colossians will be encouraged by Paul's own cruciform suffering on their behalf, with the result that the Colossians will be united by a love of this sort among themselves, following the model of the Christlike, others-focused, "suffering on behalf of the other" love exhibited by Paul toward them.

Paul's encouragement models cruciform love and enables unity in both its enactment and its reception. Being knit together in love would result, Paul continues, in the church's arrival at the knowledge of God's mystery—namely, Christ. Thus once again we encounter the logic that moves from works of communal, active, reciprocal cruciform love in the church to a revelation of the knowledge of who God is in Christ. Without the communal aspect (namely, the unity) and without the love (that which itself makes the unity possible), the knowledge of God is incomplete.[9]

A few verses later (Col 2:6-8), Paul exhorts believers as a plural entity to walk in Christ (Col 2:1) based on the fact that they have, as a plural entity, been rooted in Christ.[10] This will result in their bearing fruit and being established in Christ (Col 2:7). The theme of incorporation into

Christ continues in Colossians 2:19, where we are told that those who are under Christ the head are thereby included in his body and are knit together. Here Paul uses the same verbal root ("knit together") as in Colossians 2:1-2, where the unity came through love. Unity and support as a part of the one body under Christ leads to a communal growth "with the growth that comes from God." Just like the corporate metaphor in Colossians 3:10—where the plurality of believers exists in the singular reality of the new man (i.e., Christ)—Paul uses the image of growth as a body in Colossians 2:19 to communicate incorporation into the "entire body" (my translation), which in Greek is expressed through a singular phrase. This phrase refers to a corporate, plural participation in the community, grammatically spoken of and rendered in the Greek as one singular entity experiencing growth. This continues to express the Pauline teaching that the collective unity of the church as a community of shared life, worship, culture, and communion is crucial and inseparable from the individual's personal growth in holiness. This is further evidenced by the two singular participles *supported* and *united*, which contribute to the metaphor of the plural participation in one singular body experiencing growth. By utilizing the plural when referring to the joints and ligaments, through which the singular body is supported and united, Paul successfully integrates the individual into the corporate image of the church as a single body that is growing precisely through the support of others, distinct and different people united in Christ.[11] Paul sees no dichotomy between the individual and the corporate. Rather, for him, the perfection of the one obviously cannot exist without the participation in, support of, and perfection of the other.[12] This perfection, is not numerical growth (although it is, of course, not in opposition to such growth) but "a growth toward perfection."[13]

A very similar concept of individual incorporation into a new, unified entity and existence, the body of Christ, also stands out in several other books of the New Testament. In John 15, Jesus says: "I am the vine; you are the branches. Whoever abides in me and I in him, he it is that bears much fruit, for apart from me you can do nothing. If anyone does not abide in me he is thrown away like a branch and withers; and the branches are gathered, thrown into the fire, and burned" (Jn 15:5-6). Jesus continues by exhorting his disciples to abide in his love by keeping his commandments and loving one another (Jn 15:9-10, 12-14). Likewise, in 1 Peter 2:5, we encounter a comparable metaphor of individual incorporation into a singular, corporate entity. There Peter envisions the church to be like "living stones" that "are being built up as a spiritual house, to be a holy priesthood, to offer spiritual sacrifices acceptable to God through Jesus Christ" (1 Pet 2:5). This singular spiritual house consists of a multitude of living stones and has Jesus Christ himself as the cornerstone (1 Pet. 2:6-8). The corporate temple theme of Peter is comparable to what we find in Ephesians: the mystery of God is revealed to be the fact that Jews and Gentiles, though formally separated, are now included in the "one new man" (Eph 2:15) and the "same body" (Eph 3:6). This body is also described in Ephesians, like in 1 Peter, through the concept of the believers constituting a household (Eph 2:19) and a temple (Eph 2:21) built on Jesus Christ the cornerstone (Eph 2:20). Of course, elsewhere in Paul the theme and reality of the unity of the body of Christ evidences this same commitment to a collective incorporation into a singular entity, the body of Jesus Christ himself.[14]

Returning to Colossians 3, verses 12-14 make it clear that incorporation into the new man, Jesus Christ, includes an entire pattern of life believers are to adopt and live out. It is worth noting that each of the virtues listed is elsewhere attributed to God and to Jesus Christ. Thus in exhorting the believers as a plural entity (the imperatival form ["put on"] is plural) to put on the virtues, all of which are grammatically singular, Paul indicates that this is not a matter of a multitude of individual sanctification projects occurring in the same location as a sort of Christian self-help group. Rather, this is a communal transformation—a cruciformation—that takes place by inhabiting and imitating the cruciform God.[15] We are cruciformed through our Christlike participation in the community of Christ's love embodied, enacted, and received. By faith and baptism, we "put on" Christ, which is a reference not simply to a new identity but an invitation and exhortation to become like Jesus both in the midst of and due to one's involvement in the life, worship, and witness of the community (Col 3:12, 14).[16]

Love as the Communal Bond that
Leads to Perfection

In Colossians 3:14, Paul returns to the idea of the perfection of the believers in and through the church via love. The ESV translates this verse, "And above all these [referring to the preceding virtue list] put on love, which binds everything together in perfect harmony." Such a translation, however, wrongly assumes that "love" is supposed to function as a belt of sorts in the clothing metaphor, somehow binding all of the other virtues together. A more accurate translation would be, "governing/controlling all of these things is love." Such a rendering recognizes that the Greek preposition *epi* here is not simply indicating that love is "above" all of the rest of the Christian moral virtues in terms of degree (though that is true as well), but that all of Christian life, worship, and virtue is empowered and activated by cruciform love as a transformative force or energy.

This love governs, controls, enables all of the other virtues as a power, and it thereby creates a bond between believers that leads to their perfection. While there are a variety of interpretations of the Greek phrase *ho estin syndesmos tēs teleiotētos* (lit. "which is the bond of perfection"), the most convincing interpretation in the larger context of Colossians is the one that envisions love as a communal bond between the congregants that results in perfection.[17] In light of Colossians 1:28 making the aim "perfection" in Christ, and most especially in the usage of the same Greek term ("bond") in Colossians 2:19—where it is in the plural and clearly refers to the bond that holds the entire body together—it is highly likely that the sense here is along the same lines. Therefore, Paul's point thus far is that through the enactment and reception of love in the church, we encounter the God who is love. This encounter and embodiment of cruciform love binds believers together in the one new man, Jesus Christ, so that Christ might be all and in all.

Cruciform Perfection Through the Melodic
and Harmonic Ministry of the Word

While all of the above could contribute as much to a theology of moral formation and sanctification as it does to the topic of worship, what Paul says in Colossians 3:16 specifically invokes the theme of singing as a mechanism by which the power and person of Christ is made ecclesially present. This presence comes about through the word about Christ as it is expressed in worship through psalms, hymns, and spiritual songs. In my own translation of Colossians 3:16, I rendered it as follows: "Let the word of Christ abundantly make a home among you with all wisdom by means of teaching and admonishing one another, through psalms, hymns, and spiritual songs, by means of singing them with your hearts to God through the grace of reciprocity."

Rarely do I come across pastors, church ministers, or worship leaders (or even congregations) who speak about the ministry of music as a ministry of the Word. In fact, if you were to ask pastors at random about the mechanism by which admonition and teaching takes place, it is highly probable that the first answer from most of them would be "in the preaching." For some, preaching would be the only place where teaching is done in the church. Yet while Paul would certainly affirm that the preaching of the Word is a powerful and primary means of transformative worship in the way of the cross, the fact remains that in Colossians 3:16 (and in its parallel in Ephesians 5:18-20), the ministry of musical worship is an additional powerful means by which people are both filled with the Spirit (Eph 5:19) and filled with the word about Christ (Col 3:16). I would go so far as to say that, based on these verses, singing as a liturgical activity is co-equal with preaching in terms of its Spirit-governed potential to bind the community together—through expressing God's love to one another aloud; through participating as a community in an aesthetic creation; through sharing melody, harmony, and poetry as a believing body of Christ.

An analysis of the verse reveals that the word about Christ (Gk. literally "word of Christ"), which is admittedly a vague phrase, refers to the traditions and teachings of the church about the person and work of Christ, specifically, his gospel work in the redemption of the world through his life, death, and resurrection. This "word about Christ" dwells ("makes a home," or "takes up residence") in the church by means of singing. The Greek participle (lit. "singing") is an adverbial participle of means, which is Greek geek speak for saying that it expresses the means by which the word about Christ dwells in the church: namely, through or by singing psalms, hymns, and spiritual songs. Furthermore, I propose that the prepositional phrase *en tē chariti* (lit. "in grace") should be translated more along the lines of "in the reciprocity of grace" rather than more neutrally as "with gratitude" (ESV). My translation of the Greek word *charis* ("grace") brings out the radical gracious reciprocity that occurs in the context of communal singing, which is actually part of the sense of the Greek word in antiquity. Through hearing the gospel sung from the other, and from singing the gospel to the other, the God of the gospel, Jesus Christ, is made audibly, aesthetically, and personally present by the power of the Holy Spirit. We experience a revelation and an encounter with the living God through song by which the Spirit knits us together through the melodic, harmonic, and poetic embodying of Jesus Christ, the sonic sanctifier and perfecter of our souls. When this happens, we together begin to experience a cruciformation into the family resemblance of the cruciform God.

Again, when we sing about Jesus, we are not simply delivering content about him through a neutral medium. In a real sense, to cite Marshall McLuhan, "The medium is the message."[18] We are not communicating a list of abstract ideas about Jesus through the pedagogical tool of hymns so that we might sing doctrines about Jesus and pass the theology litmus test of the pearly gates. Rather, when we sing the gospel, we are making present the living Christ in the midst of his body, experiencing him aesthetically in real time through each other, witnessing the unity of the triune God through the unity of our voices in harmony, and encountering him as and through the community. Thereby we are transformed into his image by his presence with us from one degree of glory to the next.[19]

CONCLUSION: CRUCIFORMATION AS WORSHIP IN THE WAY OF THE CROSS

I have argued that the practices, people, and customs of our lives, both inside and outside of the church, contribute to the cultures in which we live and move and have our being. By the very nature of our existence, we find ourselves at once shaped by the worlds we inhabit and shapers of the world for better or worse. The same has been shown to be true for the church. While the worlds that we inhabit often operate according to the myths of violence and individualism, the narrative world of the church is empowered by the narrative of the cruciform way of God in Jesus Christ, experienced through its enactment and reception through the body.

For Paul, cruciformation occurs through walking in the way of God and worshiping with the people of God. Worship in the way of the cross, cruciformation, is meant to conform us to the family resemblance of God. This is accomplished by embodying God's love through God's loving community whereby we become like the God who is love. It is all about being transformed by, through, and into Christlike character through the community by which we are cruciformed. Through the mode and medium of music, we are renewed by love into the image of the cruciform God. Love can exist only where there is an other. We can only be rooted in love where there is both an other to love, and another by whom we might be loved.

Worship is neither a performance for God nor is it a form of therapy for us. Rather, worship is the disposition of a church who is being transformed by the image of the God of love as we gaze at his glory in the face of Jesus Christ through one another.

6

AN APOLOGY FOR THE CHURCH

Before moving on to the application of the theology of cruciformation to the various elements of worship in the church, I feel that it is necessary to make an apology for the church. I use the word *apology* in both the traditional and colloquial sense of the term. This chapter is both an expression of regret on behalf of the failings of the church and a justification for my defense of the vital importance of the church.

CHURCH APOLOGIES

If we say we love Jesus, we must also by necessity love the church. The church is the body of Christ and we are members of his body both in local congregations and in global fellowship. For many of us, the love of the church does not come easily. This is undoubtedly a result of the fact that the church contains people. Ah, yes, people—a constant source of problems! If there were no people in the church then the idea of burden-bearing, loving one another, and acting in humility and others-centered deference would not be such a challenging concept. Yet if we're honest, when we as a culture say things like, "We love Jesus, but not the church," we are speaking about the difficult reality of living in community with other human beings, whether Christian or not. Whether unlovable, annoying, cruel, narcissistic, and uninspiring or, on the other hand, imaginative, hopeful, humble, peaceful, and inspirational, we have all surely encountered people of each of these descriptions both in the world and in the church.

Our experience in and as the church, and our perception of the church as a theological idea and ideal can become incredibly frustrated and convoluted when we are forced to come to grips with the fact that the people who comprise the church are often what make us hate the church the most. We love Jesus, and not only do we not love the church, oftentimes we positively can't stand it. We wish we could love it, but we doubt with all its complexities and hypocrisies that it will ever become lovable enough to win our affections. Indeed, we see the church as a part of the problem, not as a part of the solution. We see the church as a stumbling block in the way to Christ rather than his body. We must first be willing to be honest about why we are skeptical about the church (from a human perspective) so that we might develop a true, biblically informed affection for the church, which is the temple of the Holy Spirit, the body of Christ, the household of the faith, and the pillar and foundation of truth.[1]

How do these two seemingly polar opposite patterns of thought—a suspicion, apathy, and skepticism of the church and a call to love it—fit with any sort of cohesion in the same mind and practice? I would argue that the person who is critical of the subculture of the church may, in fact, be justified in that critique while still being called to cultivate and embody the cruciform love of Jesus in, through, and from the people of God, the body of Christ, the church. Furthermore, I propose that in actuality it is not the church according to the Bible that you, I, or anyone claims to dislike; rather, more often the church according to our perception of church—that is, a conglomeration of various subcultural elements to which we give the name *church*—is rightfully rejected by many followers (and critics) of Jesus.

This distinction between competing visions of the church—as a hodgepodge of various subcultural elements labeled *church* versus a biblical, New Testament vision of the church—is crucial to this chapter, where I am calling us to love both Jesus and his people and body, the church. It is often the case that worship leaders, when they hear "you must love the church" think of the subcultural hodgepodge church rather than the biblical church. Thus when they find themselves critical of, turned off by, or even disdaining certain subcultural distinctions that they associate with "the church," they interpret this as a crisis of vocation and possibly even a crisis of faith. I remember, as a young evangelical leader, hearing that when someone "gets saved" you know they have experienced a conversion by observing the fruit of the Spirit. But instead of turning to the actual virtues listed in Galatians, this particular minister enumerated an entirely different list of authenticating virtues including these: a love for Bible studies; an unceasing love for prayer meetings and modern worship music; an immovable trust in religious leaders in the church and a "natural" agreement with practically everything they ever preach and teach; and a strong desire to be involved in programmatic small groups in which people "do life."[2] The problem with such instruction is that it confuses a biblical theology of the church with a subcultural conglomeration of churchy things, like Bible studies and programmatic small groups. The latter view of the church is constituted by phenomenological data, including elements that a worship leader can legitimately love, hate, or be indifferent toward; but the former—namely, a biblical view of the church—demands our affections and our cruciform participation. When I insist that worship leaders love both Jesus and his church, I am always referring to the biblical, rather than the merely cultural, view of the church.

I exhort you, brothers and sisters, to love Christ's body, the church, with the same vigor, zeal, and passionate hearts with which you love Christ himself. There is no love of God in isolation, because to know the love of God is to experience his love (which is his very nature) through enacting his love toward and receiving his love from other people. In Ephesians, Paul exhorts the church in this manner, saying, "Husbands should love their wives as their own bodies. He who loves his wife loves himself. For no one ever hated his own flesh, but nourishes and cherishes it, just as Christ does the church, because we are members of his body" (Eph 5:28-30).

To hate the body of Christ is to hate Christ. To hate the biblical view of the church as the community of sinners set apart to be saints through the instantiation of divine love is to hate yourself, because you, as a Christian, no longer exist apart from Christ and his body. Whoever is in Christ and a member of his body by baptism is a new creation; the old is passed and the new has come (2 Cor 5:17; Gal 6:15). Joined to his body we should be able to say with Paul, "I have been crucified with Christ. It is no longer I who live, but Christ who lives in me" (Gal 2:20). Jesus himself exhorts his disciples to abide in the vine, in him, and thus in his love. He then immediately explicates this saying by noting that abiding in his love is accomplished by keeping his commandments. The primary commandment Jesus gives is "love one another as I have loved you" (Jn 15:12).

A biblical theology of cruciformation and worship in the way of the cross is all about our renewal through knowledge of God into the image of God, our Creator. It takes place communally through love within the body of Christ. Love itself is spoken of as the bond that binds us together in the church (cf. Col 3:14), perfects us, and reveals to us not merely knowledge about God but a personal, existential, communal, and intimate knowledge of and encounter with God himself, by love, through the other (see e.g. 2 Cor 12:9; Col 1:28-29; Jas 1:4; 1 Jn 4:18). In and through this reciprocal love in the context of the church, we are "being renewed in knowledge after the image of [the] creator" (Col 3:10). Thus whatever cultural, ethnic, and socioeconomic distinctions we bring with us into the body, through this localized incarnation of divine, cruciform love, Christ is "all and in all" (Col 3:11; cf. Gal 3:28).

To hate the church as defined by Holy Scripture is to hate Christ and to hate oneself. The old "you" (sg.) died, so that the new "you" (pl.) can live and walk in newness of life—reconciled, redeemed, and experiencing communal renewal in the image of the God who is love, through the energizing component of faith, love.[3] The heartbeat, soul, lifeblood, and sustaining energy of the church is the love of God in, with, and through Jesus Christ, experienced communally in, with, and through one another. There is no life or fruit-bearing outside of the vine, there is only death and a pile of dead, useless, and fragmented twigs. There are no individuals who are being saved as salvation-solo-projects in the kingdom of God; there are only interconnected members of the body whose spiritual sustenance, salvation, and renewal are contingent upon their very connectedness and mutual dependence in the body. Without the other we are not the body of Christ but rather a box full of amputated limbs lying lifelessly in the same location. With the other, we are a body in desperate need of the lifeblood of love, which joins us together and grows us up in

Christ, through Christ, as the body of Christ. As one church father put it: "There is no salvation outside of the Church."[4]

Relatedly, it is because of the sheer value of human life in particular (whether Christian or not) as made in the image and likeness of God that people—as difficult or wonderful as they may be according to their various dispositions—are of supreme value and infinite worth. If love is the means by which people (especially the church) are renewed in the image of God and encounter Jesus, then every time that we as Christians incarnate and exhibit the love of God, every time we care for someone, bind their wounds, bear their burdens, and sacrificially pour ourselves out for them, that person is encountering the living God through us. Every act that issues forth from a heart governed by the cruciform love of God demonstrates and images God's own character, redemption, and new creation. The heart of God is most clearly demonstrated through the person and work of Jesus Christ. For God loved the world in this manner, that he gave his only Son that whoever believes in him may not perish but have everlasting life (Jn 3:16). If the heartbeat of God, the Creator of the world, is for the salvation and life of the world—all of it—then we must embody that love, pursue that love, enact that love, and in so doing, be ourselves transformed through that love, into the image of the God who himself is love, Jesus Christ.

CRUCIFORM FAMILY

On account of a biblical theology which recognizes the glory and worth of humanity as created in the image and likeness of God, we must pursue a deep, transcendent, empathetic, new-creation love for people. It is not uncommon in our culture to view our blood relatives as our true family and our other close friends and the church as a family in a purely meta-phorical sense. Consequently, while we would do anything for our natural brothers and sisters because they are blood, there is often not the same sense of intense commitment to our non-blood-related brothers and sisters, with whom we work and live, and in particular, with whom to-gether we constitute the family of God, the church. Thus, while it is rare and the result of extreme circumstances that natural family members become estranged, estrangement from the family of God, the church—

perhaps in part because it is viewed as merely metaphorical family membership—is common and considered to be a normal privilege of our prerogative as consumers of the Christian religion. The frequency with which our Christian culture shops for a new church and the laxity with which we embark on this endeavor indicates that we have an insufficient view of the church as a community of people, a family, consisting of the adopted children who are being cruciformed into a family resemblance with the triune God. Russell Moore has written:

> Adoption, into a family or into the Family of God, is "real." There is no such thing in God's economy as an "adopted child," only a child who was adopted into the family. "Adopted" defines how you came into the household, but it doesn't define you as some other sort of family member. In the Book of Romans, Paul defines all Christians, both Jew and Gentile, as having received a common "spirit of adoption" (Rom. 8:15; 9:4).[5]

What if we started to view our fellow human beings as those whom God is desiring to adopt into the family of redemption, the church? And what if we began to view our brothers and sisters in the church not as metaphorical, lesser siblings, able to be cast off at the first sign of social friction, but as our not blood-related but blood-bought, Spirit-filled, true and real family? Then the thought of leaving a church for a better children's program, or as the result of a desire for fresher worship, or because of a quarrel with a fellow adopted sibling of God would seem less like a change of preferential worship location and more like the excruciatingly painful tearing apart of body parts, the pulverizing of joints, and the laceration of the ligaments of the body of Christ.

We need to love the church and its people with such zeal that the thought of its rupture or schism is devastating to our inmost being, rather than merely incidental. Viewing our neighbor, both inside and outside of the church, as true family—with the same potential for vulnerability and closeness that comes in the natural family—will assist us in developing a biblical, Christlike affection for humanity in general, and for the people of God in particular (cf. Gal 6:10; 1 Tim. 4:10). When we achieve this awareness and begin to experience it in the world, the depths to which we will go for the life and salvation of the world—for other people—will be endless and governed by an abiding and relentless hope, peace, and unity that surpasses understanding.

While the evangelical tradition has typically been excellent with calling all people to salvation in Christ alone and to subsequently engaging converts in worship and biblical piety, it has historically not been as strong in regard to its ecclesiology, its theology of the church. However, we can't have Jesus without the church and without people. We can have the church without preconceived churchy programs marked by subcultural quirks, but we can't have Jesus without the church, and we can't have the church without Jesus. In fact, the primary way we are given to encounter Jesus is through people and through the bearing of the burdens of the other. Thus the starting point to any ministry in the church is the cultivation of a paradoxical love for the church: a love that exists not in spite of the things that challenge and annoy us about humanity but that is present precisely and most profoundly through them.

The church will never be lovable enough to win our affections from a human perspective, but the gospel redefines what it means to be human, and thereby redefines both what it means to love and what it means to be the church. The church isn't a subcultural set of styles, preferences, or approaches, and the church is not a building; rather, it is a body. Without the body we have nothing. Without the body we're lifeless, amputated limbs. Without the body, we can't know love or know God in intimate and abiding ways, because without the body of Christ, we don't have Jesus. As we move on and seek to consider how to minister zealously in the ecclesial setting to congregants and to other ministry leaders, consider the words of the classic hymn "The Church's One Foundation":

> The Church's one foundation is Jesus Christ her Lord;
> she is his new creation, by water and the word:
> from heaven he came and sought her to be his holy bride;
> with his own blood he bought her, and for her life he died.
> Elect from every nation, yet one o'er all the earth,
> her charter of salvation, one Lord, one faith, one birth;

one holy Name she blesses, partakes one holy food,

and to one hope she presses, with every grace endued.

Yet she on earth hath union with God, the Three in one,

and mystic sweet communion with those whose rest is won.

O happy ones and holy! Lord, give us grace that we

like them, the meek and lowly, on high may dwell with thee.[6]

CONCLUSION: A CALL TO ECCLESIAL, CRUCIFORM ACTION

This chapter is not meant to function as an abstract proclamation about the idea of the church; it is intended to be an exhortation to us all to be the church. It is rather simple to theologize about the church, but it is much harder to creatively guide those ideas into action. Christ did not die for propositions about people; he died for people. And he intends to call all people to himself through a particular, called, redeemed, and reconciled people, the church. Therefore, this chapter is not just a lecture, it is a call. It is a call to be the church, to love the church, to revitalize the church, to reform the church, and thereby to become reconciled to Christ through the church so that we might become reconcilers for Christ as the church. In the remaining sections of this book, a theology of worship in the way of the cross—cruciformation—will be applied to the practical elements of worship, ministry, and life in and as the church.

Becoming a cruciformed church requires a commitment to cruciform creativity from the heart of the local congregation for the good of our communities. One way we can pursue that goal is by seeking to be cultivators of culturally rich art that transforms our communities and our very selves from the heart of the local church.

None of this is easy, but all of it is necessary, because with, in, and as the body of Christ we can do all things, but apart from Christ and apart from one another, we can do nothing. There are many worthy causes and revolutions to be fought in the human sphere, and we should vigorously engage in them. However, the one revolution that ungirds them all is the gospel of Jesus Christ, who through the revolutionary power of love has defeated the daunting end and enemy of every other path to freedom and revolution in this world, death. This is a call to be an active and engaged part of that revolution by committing to the charge to be Christ's body, the church, and to reconcile the world to God through love, for love, and by love so that we might become like the God who is love, Jesus Christ.

PART 3

CRUCIFORM COUNTERCULTURE

7

WORSHIP AT THE KARAOKE CHAPEL

From Subculture of Sameness to Counterculture of Cruciformity

Three hundred fifty bucks and that's the final payment. I don't care what your deal was with Matty!" shouted Dave, the thickly bearded new manager of the Green Shamrock, a small Irish pub in the Brighton neighborhood of Boston, Massachusetts.[1] At six foot three and about 290 pounds, Dave appeared to me to be a condescending mix between a balding, rabid, malevolent, Irish American fortysomething and a Wookiee. He continued his tirade in the dialect of Irish Bostonian barking: "Look. It was a slow night. You guys didn't draw well; you get paid less. That's how it goes. End of story. Is that a problem?"

"Is it a problem? Is it a problem?" I replied, asking with an attitude in my voice that communicated in my best Bostonian tone, "I want to rip off your head and use it as a bowling ball." Getting in his face I continued, "I think it's safe to say there is a problem, Dave. And I think that problem is going to be resolved right now by you forking over the full $750. Or else [wait for it] we're going to take it outside."

"Whoa! John. Settle down, buddy. We'll sort it all out," Ben the keyboard player assured me as he raveled up the last of the instrument cables.

"Yeah. Sorry, Dave! He's had a bit to drink tonight," added our guitarist Stefan. "He didn't mean anything by it."

Meanwhile, I thought to myself, *Nonsense! Of course I meant something by it! I should keep talking. I'm doing pretty good.* I figured, *I'm already so invested in this argument, I might as well keep it going.*

"Ohhhhh, yes, I did mean something by it, Dave," I shouted, "you big idiotic oaf. I guess it's time for us to take this outside after all."

The rest of the band sighed, "Here we go!" trading nervous glances as they watched the latest rock'n'roll ruckus unfold before their very eyes.

"You might think, Dave, that you can take me down, because you're a big tall goofy clown. But I'm warning you, tough guy [channeling my inner Frank Rizzo[2]], I might not look like much but I've got a lot of heart!" I felt as though I could not be stopped and that justice must be served. This was a matter of life and death! "That's our money that we count on for food, and for gasoline for the van, man," I yelled, "How would you like it if someone started messing with your income?"

Now (truth be told) at this stage in my life, I subsisted on a meager diet consisting of a well-balanced mix of cigarettes, chicken fingers, Captain Crunch cereal, and the occasional random carrot—all the nutrients that a growing boy needs to experience holistic health. It really wasn't as if I would truly starve without the full payment, but it felt more like a matter of justice and respect.

Dave just shrugged (and probably laughed) off my noble (or pathetic) challenges for a street fight. From my perspective, however, instead of preparing for an epic battle with a worthy foe [me], Dave weaseled away, shivering in his soul from the dread brought about by my terrifying demeanor and intimidating, nearly 115-pound physique. I watched as he retreated like a coward into the back office where I imagined that he called his mommy on the phone like a big blubbering baby. "Davie got scaredy scared. Davie no wanna fightie! Davie wanna go home, eat peanut-butter sandwich, watch cartoonies!" From everyone else's perspective, however, the reality was clear. After coolly gesturing for my band to come and retrieve me and to get me under control, Dave simply shuffled off to the back room office to cash out the bar and to do the books for the night.

Well, I wasn't going to let Dave have the last word. Jumping up onto the foot rail of the bar and lifting my body up as high as I could, I got myself in the best position to rage against the machine of Dave and his systemic pub evil, which had recently become the bane of my existence, or at the very least, a source of momentary affliction due to monetary deduction. Turning to the four college-aged employees who worked in the pub I proclaimed, "Your boss Dave is a total [bleep]. And deep down, I know that you all know that what I am saying is true. Why work for such a lousy (insert long string of expletive adjectives here) cheat? Now is your chance to leave this place! To find a better life! Follow me! I'm never playing at this corrupt club ever again for that crooked son of a [bleep]. I'm out of here! Who's coming with me?"

Turning around, I was shocked to discover that no one at all was moved by my rousing, Oscar-worthy performance. To describe the response as crickets chirping would be too generous. Instead, the gentle, quiet clang of beer glasses being washed by hand and then stored away, the slight swoosh of brooms sweeping floors, and the occasional amused giggle from the bartenders were the only responses I received to my revolutionary declaration. I don't know what had gotten into me, really. I guess it was the fact that my band had just finished our weekly three-hour long, Thursday night cover gig and we were in the midst of being ripped off by this crook to the tune of $400. I of course knew that if I ended up fighting Dave I would almost certainly—barring some miracle from heaven—be pummeled and stomped into a bloody mess in the cold, icy winter streets of Brighton that night. But I had lived in New England long enough and listened to enough of the Dropkick Murphys to have it in my blood to at least give it my best dropped-out-of-college try. But honestly, I think I was itching for a fight because of the fundamentally unsatisfying nature of my "art" in those days. Something about playing Top 40 pop hits from the '70s, '80s, and '90s for three hours in a row for an audience consisting primarily of intoxicated college students makes a good old-fashioned street fight seem cathartic. Certainly I might break a few bones in the process, but I could also break my boredom.

WIND-UP WORSHIP MONKEYS IN THE KARAOKE CHAPEL

I have not told this true story about myself to glorify my former days in the depraved kingdom of nightclubs and nonsense. Soon after that time, ironically on a tour with my band funded primarily by months of savings raised from playing weekly cover gigs, I came to a true and life-changing knowledge of the gospel in Decatur, Georgia, while reading the book *The Purpose Driven Life* in the parking lot for the famous folk club Eddie's Attic right before our gig there. Thus my boast is not in my former stupidity but in my Lord and Savior, Jesus Christ. Nor, however, do I tell this story for mere entertainment purposes. Rather, I tell it because it ties into my experience as a worship leader in the church and especially to recent feelings I have been having about the homogeneity of contemporary Christian worship music and church culture.

Before you sigh and either prepare yourself to be equipped for a new battle or simply close the book, let me be clear: I am not arguing against contemporary worship music in favor of traditional organ music. Conversely, I am not arguing against organ music either, although personally whenever I hear the pipe organ I feel a sense of doom as though God wants me dead and will smite me at any moment. When I refer to homogeneity in Christian worship music and church culture, I am thinking of my experience over the years and of late in which I have witnessed the church's mistaken propensity to adopt the posture and ethos of a subculture of Christian sameness—complete with its own prepackaged and predictable music, clothing, and jargon—instead of a counterculture of cruciformity that looks different in each place and that is more chaotic and real, and compellingly creative and transformative. I'll parse this out in more detail in the next chapter, but for the moment it is worth noting a bit of the background for this part of the discussion. My general argument is that because of the subcultural commitment of the church (at least in North America) to a form of artistic pragmatism and self-imposed stylistic pigeonholing, the church in musical worship is beginning to feel like a karaoke bar in which we perform cover songs for Christ.

Assuming that what I have argued thus far has at least some truth to it—that is, there is a real sense in which through active participation in and as the church we are transformed through love into the image of the God who is love—it follows that a major aim of Christian communal life and worship is the transformation of the believer into the image of God through the other. I find this transformational component to ecclesial life to be one of the most exciting elements of worship when it involves diverse peoples coming together into one local body, not as a melting pot in which to lose their individuality and identity in favor of a lowest common denominator culture of sameness, but as a richly creative and complex matrix of mutual blessing. However, when I come into contact with the actual church as it exists—not in my head, but as it is in the real world—I find myself deeply disturbed by the extent to which God-ordained diversity is often traded for the human imposition of homogeneity, where creative, indigenous artistry yields to complacent replication and imitation of the Christian worship industry's status quo.

A few months ago, as I was leading a worship music set with the popular (and great) song "Better Is One Day," I felt a convicting sense of emptiness and boredom. It had nothing to do with the song per se. On the contrary, I am a big fan of the song as a piece of worship art. My feeling had more to do with the fact that, in that particular moment, in the midst of the worship service, I realized that my heart was not in it and that I was merely going through the motions. Now, in one sense, this can be fine. No worship leader always feels everything they play in deeply emotionally satisfying ways. After all, it is not ultimately about us and our feelings but about the abiding truth of the gospel and the glory of God by which he intends to transform the world through the church.

Yet what really bugged me about this particular episode of worship apathy was that during it, I had an epiphany concerning the reason I felt so empty inside in the midst of the moment. In this case, I realized that my dissatisfaction arose not simply because I wasn't into the music or because I was distracted, but rather it was rooted in the realization that twelve years after my cover gig apocalypse at the Green Shamrock, I was still (to my horror) doing cover gigs. But now instead of playing cover gigs for a crowd of drunk college students, I was playing cover gigs for a congregation, and worse: I was playing cover gigs for God! I felt like one of those wind-up toy monkeys with the cymbals that plays children's songs. The only difference was that this monkey, when wound up, played stock worship tunes in a Top 40 Christified Karaoke Chapel.

Something inside of me realized that the experience and selections I had chosen to play that morning in Phoenix, Arizona, were also being played in the same way, with the same arrangements, likely with the same effect, all over the country. And I didn't feel united to the church because of this shared experience; I felt absorbed into the sameness of it all and embarrassed at its predictability in terms of art. I was merely the mechanism, the deliverer, and the local disseminator of highly effective content crafted by somebody else, somewhere else, for someone else. I was the local distributor of the corporate product of worship delivered right to the doorstep of the individual worshiper, guaranteed to make them feel good (or their money back!). After the service, I was further disturbed when I realized that this approach did not seem at all indigenous to my particular locale. It did not arise from my own local situation and was not working itself out organically, truly, and freely from a place of authentic creativity. Rather, it appeared to me to be like an insidious, superimposed grid which predefined how true Christian community and worship should look and feel. The grid dictated in advance precisely how the Christian encounter with God in the church should be delivered, shaped, and experienced. The only difference between playing Goo Goo Dolls cover tunes at the Boston bar and contemporary Christian hits in the local church was the venue and the audience.

Why did this feel like a rank-and-file, cut-and-paste Christianity that viewed community as a corporate structure in which to be assimilated into sameness rather than an organic and unpredictable body in which to grow together through cruciformational worship? Why did this approach to worship feel like something invented by modern business executives as a strategy to grow churches and experience "successful" worship? I became convinced that we, the theological artists of the church, can do better than to simply co-opt the art of the world and either re-present it in the form of a cover tune or emulate it by adopting its form while Jesusfying its content.[3]

CONCLUSION: FROM SUBCULTURE OF SAMENESS TO COUNTERCULTURE OF CRUCIFORMITY

The gospel calls us to a more creative, more empathetic, more intuitive, more organic, local, and public body than the contemporary church as a whole has lived into in the midst of the world thus far. The church's worst enemy is often herself, and her abiding crutch and stumbling stone is her own lack of creativity and subcultural complacency. There is a way beyond the package deal of popular Christian faddishness and cut-and-paste community programming; a place that is defined by a people walking in the way of the cross, worshiping the crucified and resurrected God, and experiencing a cruciformation through the transformative enactment of Jesus' love toward the other and the reception of Christ's love from the other; a community constructed not on the precept of subcultural sameness but on the principle of countercultural cruciformity.

The subculture of sameness can never conform us to the image of God through cruciformational life and worship because the cruciform love of God—which constitutes God's very nature—requires an other to love, one who is different from us. Love for those who are like us requires no sacrifice and thus does not really even qualify as genuine love. That is better thought of as a form of narcissistic worship of the self. Love for those who are other than us and different from us requires and empowers acting out a sacrificial, cruciform love of God from us to the other and from the other to us. In the midst of that experience of divine love, we embody and encounter the cruciform Christ and are transformed by and into his love. This entire process and nature of cruciform love issues forth from the trinitarian life of God as a God who loves both internally and eternally within the Trinity and externally toward his creation. Theologian Jürgen Moltmann identifies two elements to divine love as the essence of the Trinity: love for that which is like (i.e., intertrinitarian love) and love for that which is unlike (i.e., God's sacrificial love for his creation). Both are necessary for the phrase "God is love" to be understood in its fullest sense.[4]

The church is not meant to be a place of comfortable, quantifiable religious experiences characterized by the status quo of cover tunes for Jesus and self-directed worship. It is instead a community that subverts the status quo of the corporate product of conveyor-belt Christianity. It's a place and people with Jesus Christ himself as the cornerstone, where the relentless pursuit of the good of the other leads one into the unpredictable but ancient truth and experience of God through the other, and where people find their lives by losing them. It is a place worth living in and a community worth dying for.

8

HOW THE MANY BECOME
ONE IN CHRIST

From Homogeneous Unit to Multicultural,
Multigenerational, Countercultural Family

A quick comparison between the songs to which we gravitate exclusively in many of our churches and the top 100 of CCLI's SongSelect will reveal that a Top 40 model of worship music selection is in full effect. I am not claiming that using popular contemporary worship songs is wrong. But I am questioning whether the exclusive adoption of a Top 40 radio-style commitment to "the hits" in terms of our worship music selections might be yielding the same degree of shallow artistic depth in our congregations that we experience in our cars when we listen to Top 40 radio.

Imagine a cover band playing only the current Top 40 hits each Friday night at a local pub that you attend. After spending a few Fridays hearing the same tunes, played in the same way, over and over again, most of us would long for a greater degree of variety and a more substantial depth and display of artistry. Now imagine that you went on a road trip visiting five cities in five days along the east coast of the United States. You pull into Philadelphia and go to the pub, and you hear the exact same set of Top 40 songs you were accustomed to hearing in your hometown pub, played in the same way, to a very similar group of people, with basically the same response. Next stop is New York City, where you encounter the exact same phenomenon. And the same is true for the stops in Boston, Washington, DC, and Providence. The same songs, arranged the same way, with the same effect, in each city. I think it is safe to assume that most of us would consider such a scenario to be evidence of a lack of creativity and a disturbing commitment to pragmatism as a replacement for true art.

Strange as it seems, this is precisely the pattern of cover-band Christian worship that we consider normative in the church. In addition to playing the same, latest music across geographical locations, an entire Christian media industry exists which operates to a niche market that is so financially lucrative that even non-Christians are increasingly interested in partnering with Christian companies. They do this not because they care about or are impressed with the art—after all, it is more often than not a derivative, cheesier version of what the world has already been doing better for some time—but because creating "Christian" film or music automatically injects these companies into an easily marketable, growing media demographic characterized by a very responsive and reliable consumer base.

The Homogeneous Unit Principle and Contemporary Christian Music

This move toward homogeneity in Christian art and worship mirrors an earlier trend in church planting methodology developed by Donald A. McGavran called the Homogeneous Unit Principle (hereafter HUP).[1] The HUP was an approach to church planting that focused on starting churches that ministered to people who were "demographically similar." According to David Swanson in a 2010 article in *Leadership Journal* entitled "Down with the Homogeneous Unit Principle?" the HUP states that "it is easier for people to become Christians when they must cross few or no racial, linguistic, or class barriers." Swanson notes that "ideally, then, these new churches were led by pastors whose culture, class, and skin color closely matched those of their flocks."[2] McGavran explains that the homogeneous unit can be "a culture or a language, as in the case of Puerto Ricans in New York City or Chinese in Thailand" or "a tribe or caste, as in the case of Jews in the United States, Brahmans in India, or Uhunduni in the highlands of Irian (West New Guinea)."[3] The essential strategy of the HUP, then, is to pursue gospel mission primarily within the unique units of cultural sameness in particular cultures and regions rather than seeking to conduct multicultural worship from churches that are comprised of a variety of socioeconomic, cultural, and ethnic backgrounds.[4] While McGavran did not envision HUP mission planting focused on narrow segments of people groups the final picture of the kingdom of God, the approach has been heavily criticized by missiologists and theologians precisely because of the way it forces into too narrow a stream the diverse picture of the church at worship described in the Bible.[5]

The apostle Paul, for example, exhibits the variegated and diverse yet qualitatively equal nature of the members of the church in several different epistles. Writing to the church at Galatia, Paul proclaimed an egalitarian gospel of inclusion:

> For as many of you as were baptized into Christ have put on Christ. There is neither Jew nor Greek, there is neither slave nor free, there is no male and female, for you are all one in Christ Jesus. And if you are Christ's, then you are Abraham's offspring, heirs according to promise. (Gal 3:27-29)[6]

Likewise, in Rome, a region in which we know at least some churches consisted of a mix of Jews and Gentiles, Paul wrote against ethnically based boasting in favor of a celebration of the inclusion of Jews and Gentiles as equal members of the one family of Abraham (Rom 3:27-30; 4:16).[7] In the epistle to the Galatians, Paul directly confronts and opposes Peter, even referring to Peter's ethnocentrism—evidenced by his separating of himself from eating with Gentile Christians when other Jews were around—as hypocritical, as worthy of condemnation, and "not in step with the truth of the gospel" (Gal 2:14).[8]

Elsewhere in Scripture the theme of racial, ethnic, and socio-economic inclusion into the one people of God is further highlighted and affirmed as the aim of the gospel. In the book of Revelation we encounter a vision of a multiethnic, eschatological worship service in which people from "every tribe and language and people and nation" are singing together a new song in worship to God (Rev 5:9-10). In a later scene, the heavenly worship of the eschaton clearly consists of a diverse group of human beings united by the Spirit for worship of the living God:

> After this I looked, and behold, a great multitude that no one could number, from every nation, from all tribes and peoples and languages, standing before the throne and before the Lamb, clothed in white robes, with palm branches in their hands, and crying out with a loud voice, "Salvation belongs to our God who sits on the throne, and to the Lamb!" (Rev 7:9-10)

The Hebrew Bible (Old Testament) prophesies of a time when the nations will flood to Zion and worship the one God of Israel. The prophet Isaiah writes thus in Isaiah 60:

> Arise, shine, for your light has come,
> and the glory of the LORD has risen upon you.
> For behold, darkness shall cover the earth,
> and thick darkness the peoples;
> but the LORD will arise upon you,
> and his glory will be seen upon you.
> And nations shall come to your light,
> and kings to the brightness of your rising. (Is 60:1-3)

> Violence shall no more be heard in your land,
> devastation or destruction within your borders;
> you shall call your walls Salvation,
> and your gates Praise.
> The sun shall be no more
> your light by day,
> nor for brightness shall the moon
> give you light;
> but the LORD will be your everlasting light,
> and your God will be your glory. (Is 60:18-19)

Jesus himself, in the Gospel of Luke, tells the parable of the good Samaritan, the entire point of which is obviously to prohibit limiting the exercise of ministry and the love of neighbor to those who belong to our own ethnic, socioeconomic, or geographical sphere of life. In addition to prohibitions against ethnocultural exclusion and spiritual segregation in the church, Jesus makes it abundantly clear that the kingdom and family of God consists of a variety of age groups in communion together. When the disciples ask Jesus in Mark 9:36 who would be the greatest in the kingdom, Jesus welcomes and embraces a child to demonstrate the inclusion of children in the kingdom of God. In fact, Jesus responds, "Whoever receives one such child in my name receives me, and whoever receives me, receives not me but him who sent me" (Mk 9:37). The verb translated "received" here is more helpfully translated "to welcome" and is often used in the New Testament in reference to the act of hospitality through welcoming guests into one's home (cf. Mt 10:14; Lk 16:4; Jn 4:45; Gal 4:14; Col 4:10; Heb 11:31). A few verses later, Jesus warns his hearers, "Whoever causes one of these little ones who believe in me to sin, it would be better for him if a great millstone were hung around his neck and he were thrown into the sea" (Mk 9:42).

While the practice of the inclusion of children in the covenant community has its roots in Judaism (cf., e.g., Gen 17:9-14; Ps 128), the general cultural outlook of Jesus' time was quite low in regard to children. Thus Jesus' support of—better, his mandate for—the inclusion of children in the family of God is a countercultural act of subversive inclusion in his first century context. And this is not the first time or the last time that Jesus breaks the cultural code and invites the weak and despised into his midst. Earlier in the Gospel of Mark, Jesus healed a boy with an unclean spirit (Mk 9:14-29), the Syrophoenicean's daughter (Mk 7:24-30), and the daughter of Jairus (Mk 5:21-43). It makes all the sense in the world that the cruciformation of the familial community of God's love would include children and invite children themselves to embody the love of God. Cruciformation is a formative experience that works through love to conform the church into a family resemblance with the God who is love; children belong to that family.

Children—and particularly female children—were considered to be fairly worthless in the pagan ancient world, with female infants often being left on top of trash heaps to die of exposure. In contrast to this monstrous distain for children, Jesus frames his entire teaching about the kingdom of God around children, including children, and inviting adults to become childlike in their faith in God. The Greek word used by Jesus in Mark 9:37 is not the word *teknon*, the word John and Paul often use to refer to children and to adult Christian believers as a metaphorical familial term of endearment and affection. Rather, the term Jesus uses here is actually *paidion*, which refers specifically to little children and often to newborn infants. Thus, unlike certain abortion "providers" and executives in America who can have dismal and disgusting conversations about the sale of fetal body parts from late-term abortions over dinner, Jesus is a pro-children Lord of a pro-children kingdom; a kingdom in which the young are viewed not as liabilities or disturbances but as a blessing from God and as valuable members of the community. Jesus' response is based not only on the fact that all human beings are created in the image and likeness of Almighty God (Gen 1:27), and not only on the legal prohibition of murder in the Ten Commandments (Ex 20:1-17; cf. Deut 5:4-21), but on the rich heritage of Holy Scripture that testifies to the sacredness of human life at any age under the sovereign providence of God.[9]

Following the lead of the Lord, the apostle Peter preaches that the promise of baptism and salvation is "for you and for your children" (Acts 2:38-40). And later, in Acts 16:30-34, an entire household is baptized on the basis of the conversion and faith of that household's father. Whether we believe that children were in the house or not, and whether or not we support the practice of infant baptism, nevertheless, all Christians agree in children's inclusion within the covenant community, their nurture, their value, and their infinite worth as human beings created in the image of God. The hope, of course, is that through their participation in the loving community of God, they will come to resemble the loving character of the family to which they belong.

Yet I wonder if the way that the church behaves in its practice is commensurate with Jesus' high view of children and their inclusion in the kingdom. The custom of creating multiple, simultaneous services—a pre-K-8 service, a middle school service, a high school service, and an adult service—seems to be at odds with the familial nature of the kingdom and the church. Just as it is healthy for a family to eat dinner together, I wonder if we've missed the point of the church as a covenant family, relegating the place of children to a separate community within the community. I wonder how much of that is done out of a well-meaning but biblically indefensible pragmatism that views the church as an efficient provider of age-based religious goods and services. I wonder if the implications of Jesus' radical teaching—"Whoever receives one such child in my name receives me, and whoever receives me, receives not me but him who sent me" (Mk 9:37)—has registered with us or if it has been compromised by a commitment to creating successful and age-specific worship experiences that provide a product to be consumed rather than a family to which we are meant to belong.

Catch the radical nature of this teaching: Jesus is saying that the reception and welcome of a child into the midst of the community is equal to the reception of God himself. What if we applied the same pattern that Jesus articulates here to negative concepts rather than the positive theme of "reception"? Whoever fails to educate, feed, or care for one such child fails to educate, feed, or care not just for me but him who sent me. Whoever deems one such child a nonperson or a lesser person based on their age, deems not just me but him who sent me to be a nonperson or a lesser person. Whoever demeans, puts down, purposely harms, ignores, or oppresses a child—that person does these things not only to the child but also to me, and not only to me, says Jesus, but to God the Father himself.

The kingdom of sin, the kingdom of this world—what Colossians 1:13 calls the domain of darkness—thinks it is okay to murder, abuse, ignore, and look down upon children. The prochildren, childlike kingdom of God invites children, includes children, protects children, cares for children, and offers the eternal life of Jesus Christ equally to children. This is because Jesus, the Lord of the kingdom, is the one who welcomes children into his arms.[10] Do you? Is your worship so concerned with hitting one homogeneous market that it prefers age-based segregation as a strategic way of "managing" children? Is your preaching ministry so didactic and lecture-like that it would be impossible for a child to understand it even if they were of a reasonable age? Does your church ever preach a sermon directed to children rather than to adults, or would such an enterprise be considered a waste of time and unfair to the adults who want "to be fed"? I fear that we adults are gorging ourselves on the meal of the Word, while we throw spiritual scraps, leftovers, or fast food to our little ones. I'm genuinely concerned that we've devalued children and underestimated their contribution to the body of Christ by subjecting them to a dumbed-down liturgy which basically amounts to a sanctified summer-camp, Jesus-themed pizza party. Would we as leaders in the church be able to say with Jesus: "Let the little children come to me, and do not hinder them, for to such belongs the kingdom of heaven," or would we simply redirect them away from the sanctuary to the segregated holding cells of a Sunday school ecclesio-prison?[11]

It seems thus impossible to claim any serious biblical basis for the methodology of the HUP in regard to age, ethnicity, or sociocultural status even if the HUP can be shown to be helpful in terms of pragmatic church growth. This incommensurability between the teachings of Paul, Jesus, and the entire Bible and the HUP is generally recognized in the contemporary church planting and missions movements. Further, the HUP has largely been rejected in favor of other, more theologically defensible models of mission. Nevertheless, as Swanson has argued, the HUP remains covertly and perhaps unconsciously held as a reigning methodology in many church plants, even while being explicitly rejected in principle. He notes that churches today—planting to reach very specific niche people groups such as "cultural elites, the creative class, or young professionals"—are essentially operating under the HUP but applying it to new categories beyond the original units of language, ethnicity, tribe, or caste.

CONCLUSION: FROM HOMOGENEOUS UNIT TO MULTICULTURAL, MULTIGENERATIONAL, COUNTERCULTURAL FAMILY

The Homogeneous Unit Principle relates to worship in the church in a series of notable results. In churches that reject the HUP as an evangelistic and missiological methodology, the HUP often remains active in terms of the worship experience and aesthetic expression of the church. In farming out the majority of the creative components of the worship experience to "professionals," we are abdicating our responsibility to be creative theological artists. We are made in the image of the Creator God, able to be both creative and indigenous. By exclusively co-opting and assimilating the popular art predesignated as excellent by the Christian music industry, we become lazy and lethargic in our own creative abilities. The heart of the local church lacks the output of creativity it both informs and for which it is designed. Instead of intuiting the ethos, pulse, heart, and needs of our local places and converting those elements into art that images the cruciform love of God, we place our order on the corporate output of the conveyor belt of prepackaged Christian experience.

We then indiscriminately paste this artistic culture of sameness over our congregations in the name of the pragmatism of practical ministry "success." This is the musical and aesthetic equivalent of leveling a thriving historic district of a city with its quaint colonial-era buildings, one-of-a-kind local shops, diners, and stores which exude its cultural heart, and building in its place a strip mall of sameness, comprised completely of franchised chain stores, fast food restaurants, condos, and parking garages. The strip mall will not cause the culture to cease but it will through its sameness suck the spirit out of a place, neutralizing its force in the name of homogeneity, and leaving in its wake that which is entirely predictable and uninspiring. After years of living in the strip mall of sameness, the formally thriving spirit of art and creativity dissipates entirely as the slaves of the system become complacent and comfortable without access to the revolutionary inertia that used to reside in the place. People cease to be creative shapers of the world, and instead become those who are assimilated and shaped by the limited possibilities of a predetermined world of predictability and closed systems.

9

CULTIVATING A COUNTERCULTURE
OF CRUCIFORM WORSHIP

Some Basic Principles, Paradigms, and Approaches

I am not saying that all art must be unique to our places, or that we should not admire and use the greatest of Christian works of art in music in our own worship. It makes perfect sense to connect with the church from all periods of history by engaging with the best of Christian art through the ages in the context of local church worship. This is what the communion of the saints is all about! What I am challenging the church to consider—the entire church, but especially those leading as theological artists, worship leaders, and ministers—is to approach the arts in the church not as a Top 40 mix tape that is played in every location of a chain store in a one-size-fits-all manner, but as a collection of vintage records, ancient sheet music, locally produced new songs, and demo tapes of songs-in-the-making. When we play only "the hits," we experience the equivalent of hearing a collection of Top 40 singles in the worship service. A hit single, while clearly the song on an album with the most potential to reach the widest audience compared with all of the other tracks on the release, tends to have a particular quality which lends itself to being overplayed. This eventually evacuates the song of its emotional and aesthetic impact due to the frequency with which it is heard. And this is why Top 40 radio stations change their playlists every few months, relegating a good deal of their content to the one-hit-wonder bin.

We need to think of our worship sets and musical/aesthetic choices not as a collection of disconnected hit singles which burn out after heavy use, but as classic albums that contain the occasional single, but are much more complex and satisfying works of art. In the 1990s when Nirvana's major-label debut *Nevermind* was released, there was a period of about two months when I listened only to the singles on the album and completely ignored the rest of the record.[1] The singles were so infectious and amazing that I couldn't be bothered with the other "filler" tracks, which were, I assumed, obviously of lesser artistic worth and merit. However, I remember the surprising joy I experienced when I mistakenly let the cassette (yes, I know that makes me look old) play on to one of the non-single tracks called "Breed" and then to another non-single called "Polly." These were all great songs and they hung together in an artistically brilliant way. I flipped the tape and proceeded to listen to the "B sides," all of which were excellent.

From there I conducted the same experiment with all of my albums, which at the time consisted of mostly Metallica, Green Day, and Nirvana. I went from having ten to fifteen hits that I played over and over to discovering hundreds of great songs that had been there all along. But I had been conditioned to settle exclusively for the hit single. Our culture has lost the concept of the album as an art form and has been increasingly moving toward music as an ad hoc collection of random singles detached from their context.

This tendency of leaning toward the hits is basically a parallel phenomenon to the impulse in worship to play only the Top 40 on the CCLI charts. We need to adopt a view of the worship leader as the gatherer and guardian of great music and the ecclesial composer and compiler of art and worship that feels like an album (even a compilation album) rather than a non-cohesive, disparate, and disconnected collection of hit singles. Likewise, we need to return to the view of the church as a connoisseur of great art and culture.

REVIVING ART IN THE CHURCH

The church should not only steer itself away from the commercialized, cover-band, congregational-karaoke-machine approach to worship music in the local church; it should, in addition, reject the relegation of Christian art to a derivative, lesser form of art than "secular" music. Throughout various periods of history, the best art arose from the heart of the church for the worshiping community. Now, however, in many congregations, art, music, and aesthetics are merely extras that serve the sermon. They do not function in the way Paul envisions that they should—that is, as means of making present the word about Christ so that we might encounter Christ through the other and experience a cruciformation.

The church needs to put her money where her mouth is and—to be honest—to put her money where the Scriptures necessitate it be placed for the furthering of vibrant, life-changing ministry. We no longer live in a culture in which forty-five-minute, or even twenty-five-minute, didactic lecture sermons are a form of effective discourse. Leaving aside the revo-lution in preaching that needs to occur if the church is to avoid becoming either one among many "spiritual" self-help groups or an embarrassingly irrelevant vestige to the yesteryears of pious pulpiteering, the church should now be—and indeed at its best has always been—the place where people encounter Christ by the power of the Spirit, through the other, in prayer, preaching, sacrament, and song. None of these deserves to be sidelined or set out as more important.

Increasingly, it is becoming clear to me and others that the status-quo ecclesial culture and practice of vetting our preachers with a fine-toothed comb while cavalierly electing amateurs to lead a song here or there in church to give it some pizzazz needs to go. Sometimes when I mention this line of thought to preaching pastors, they react negatively by as-serting that the music ministry should be open to all levels of congre-gants as a place to serve. Aside from the fact that such a suggestion is patently absurd, unwise, and insulting to actual artists and musicians who do not view their craft as a hobby but as a carefully honed skill, it is inconsistent with most preaching pastors' own lack of willingness to allow amateur volunteers to give it their best go in the pulpit.

I advocate paying all of the church musicians weekly. This is pref-erable even when budget constraints allow for only a small stipend. When this is not possible, such as in a church plant, I recommend going with a smaller, simpler, carefully vetted worship and arts team rather than allowing a free-for-all of amateur participation in the name of "using spiritual gifts." Just as no one wants to sit through a concert full of subpar performances of music, so should it be in the church. Congregants are not entitled to positions of leadership in the church. Rather, positions of service and leadership should be thoughtfully shepherded and intentionally extended to individuals who are both called and qualified. There is a place for amateurs to hone their craft before forcing other people to suffer from their mediocrity. This place is neither the concert venue not the church sanctuary. It is, rather, their bedroom.

In arguing against cover-band worship in favor of a more creative, cruciform, countercultural ethos of Christian worship, I am not suggesting that one must always play one-hundred-percent original material to meet the criteria for artistic excellence in the church. Rather, developing a keen sense of artistic intuition in terms of musical choices, styles, and song selection and cultivating a complex aesthetic palate should be a top priority. In my view, this always involves including some mix of the best popular contemporary worship songs, hymns (both newly arranged and done in a traditional style), my own original songs, antiphons or psalms, and even a cappella metrical renderings of Scripture such as metrical psalms or other sung parts of the liturgy.[2]

To maximize the creative potential, our approach to worship should include enough freedom and space within the arrangements for improvisation and spontaneous Spirit-led creation on the spot. While we do not want to turn the worship session into a forty-five-minute, unrestrained, unorganized, Christian version of a Grateful Dead concert, there is something to be said about the power of creating new melodic and motivic material in the midst of a worship set. I refer to this as pneumatic improvisation, i.e., spiritual improvisation. Once the congregation becomes accustomed to this form of improvisational worship, they will begin intuitively contributing their own improvisational elements to the pieces, creating a lush, flowing, and free experience of worship that is completely in the moment and empowered by the Holy Spirit. Such improvisation should remain tethered to a coherent musical motif, which provides a backdrop to the new directions in melody, harmony, and spontaneous prayer. Thus music and prayer merge together in a sonic matrix of communal, doxological composition. I often tag pneumatic improvisation onto the end of a more established hymn or song. This has the effect of bringing theologically and musically excellent songs that have perhaps become stale from ecclesial overuse into a new season of fresh and worshipful congregational life.

With these suggestions, I aim only to demonstrate some of the ways that I am trying to curb the lazy impulse toward adopting a homogeneous form of Christian worship in favor of a more exciting and daring form of Christian ecclesial art. I hesitate, though, to offer any more direction than this. I fear specifically identifying a ratio of original compositions or arrangements to covers of others' work because in so doing, I would simply be reintroducing a new form of homogeneity by replacing what I see as a ubiquitous, predictable form of Christian worship with another predetermined form to be copied as the "solution." Rather, I invite readers to feel this out for themselves by applying the principle of countercultural cruciformity to their own unique congregational settings. From the heart of their particular place, they will best develop practices that result in their own contributions to fresh and creative worship and art.

Many churches are already engaged in this very task, and for that I rejoice. Worship leaders are increasingly working outside of the old world order of record labels and the worship industry, and they are creating compelling art and media from the midst of their worshiping congregations. Some of the best current examples I can think of in regard to indigenous, creative expression from the heart of the church are the musical releases of Sojourn Community Church in Louisville and projects of indie worship artist collectives like Cardiphonia (cardiphonia.org). I find that when I incorporate these noncommercial, indie works of art into my own worship sets, both the congregation and I are blessed by the refreshing experience that they bring to worship. Paradoxically, what seems to make these songs doxologically profound is their relative unfamiliarity to the congregation. Sojourn's original Advent/Christmas tune called "Hosanna in the Highest" is one of the best Christmas songs I've ever heard, and yet you will never hear it on Christian radio (thank God, lest it be corrupted by commercial oversaturation). Likewise, Cardiphonia's original modern hymn "What He to Be Our Brother Gave" is just as good as "In Christ Alone" but written by a relatively unknown layperson and released independently. Seeking these songs out takes some work, but finding them feels like uncovering a treasure. Including songs like these in worship, in conjunction with my own compositions and with some more widely known pieces, goes a long way toward contributing to a countercultural, multifaceted indigenous worship experience, transforming the karaoke chapel of cover songs for Jesus into a sanctuary of communal cruciform creativity.

T. C. MOORE, ASSOCIATE PASTOR @ NEW CITY CHURCH OF LOS ANGELES

It's Christmastide here in LA, one of the most creative cities in the world. So while this is the time of year when many evangelical churches will preach on Jesus coming into the world as the light, they will rarely preach on how Jesus and the Spirit are forming Jesus' disciples into bearers of light. The prologue of the Gospel of John says John the Baptizer was a witness to the light. And in Acts Jesus calls his disciples to be his witnesses too. In fact, Jesus calls his disciples the light of the world, a city on a hill. Yet for some reason, the evangelical church in the United States often ignores the implications of this when it comes to the way the artists and creatives in our congregations are witnesses through their artistic creativity. Evangelical Christian faith in the US can easily succumb to a form of utilitarianism that no longer recognizes how the beauty of diverse artistic expressions witnesses to the light of Christ. The light of Christ shining through diverse artistic expressions creates space for wonder and mystery and awe. And increasingly, the postmodern is discovering truth through these means. But these are rarely values of evangelical churches who instead value doctrinal correctness and certainty above all else. Perhaps that is why younger evangelicals are increasingly longing for a more sensory worship experience in liturgical traditions. Perhaps that is why millennials are increasingly dissatisfied with the dead orthodoxy of their parents' generation. Perhaps it's time for evangelicals to become bearers of the light of Jesus' good news—the "evangel"—in more ways than just preaching and singing. I would love to see God raise up more poets and sculptors and dancers in our evangelical congregations. But if God were to give these gifts to the city on a hill so they could shine for all to see, would they be welcomed and celebrated? Or would they hide under a bowl?

It is time to reject mediocrity in the musical worship in favor of a return to excellence. We must initiate a renaissance of the church as the purveyor of the best in art, culture, philosophy, and thought. The aesthetic impotency and vacuousness of contemporary worship arts should give way to local, indigenous ecclesial networks of artists—visual and digital artists, composers, songwriters, and musicians, from a variety of styles—creating fresh works of art that incarnate and make present the world-changing, reconciling gospel and bring about a transformative encounter with the person of Jesus Christ. These artist communities should be feeding creative energy into and deriving energetic inertia from the excitement and freedom that comes from places that are filled with people who refuse to be absorbed into the neutralizing vacuum of sameness propagated by church growth experts in the name of relevant and successful worship experiences. Jesus is calling the church not merely to cover Hillsong but to quite literally write, create, sing, and be empowered by a new song.[3]

CONCLUSION: THE CRUCIFIXION OF SUBCULTURAL SAMENESS THROUGH THE CRUCIFORMATIONAL COUNTERCULTURE OF THE CHURCH

In August 2013, CNN interviewed Smashing Pumpkins lead singer and guitarist Billy Corgan. When asked by CNN anchor Monita Rajpal what he was currently exploring in regard to music Corgan answered: "God . . . I think God's the great, unexplored territory in rock-and-roll music." Following up, Rajpal inquired as to what Corgan thought of "Christian rockers" to which Corgan replied with this:

> Make better music. Personally, my opinion—I think Jesus would like better bands, you know? Now I'm going to get a bunch of Christian rock hate mail . . . wait, here's a better quote—Hey, Christian rock, if you want to be good, stop copying U2. U2 already did it. You know what I mean? There's a lot of U2-esque Christian rock. Bono and company created the template for modern Christian rock. And I like to think Jesus would want us all to evolve.[4]

I completely agree. While countless excellent traditional hymns, contemporary worship songs, and iconic works of visual art have blessed and

continue to bless the church and the world, the move toward homogeneity in the worship arts precipitated by the contemporary Christian
worship industry is unwittingly creating a predictable subculture where
there should be a cruciform counterculture. The way forward is neither
to default to aesthetic conservatism by using only the hymns of past ages,
nor is it to wholeheartedly embrace the status quo of worship sameness.
Rather, as we seek to engage in the work of ministry and the worship of
Jesus in and as the church, we must reform our understanding of worship
as a cover gig for Christ and begin to view Christian art as once again an
exercise in artistic excellence from the heart of the church, for the sake
of the church, to the glory of God through the church. This can only be
accomplished when we shut down the karaoke chapel of Top 40 Jesus
hits and bring the homogeneous unit principle to the cross. There, the
cruciform love of God will transform this broken approach into a catalyst
for the communal creativity that invites the world into the wildly diverse
and unpredictable counterculture of the cruciform new creation.

PART 4

INTERPERSONAL CRUCIFORMITY

10

INTRODUCTION TO
INTERPERSONAL CRUCIFORMITY

I t was 9:00 a.m., circa 2006, on a Sunday morning in a suburban Massachusetts town just north of Boston. My eyes were closed as my mind bathed in a moment of meditative mysticism in the Spirit following the rehearsal of our worship set for the forthcoming 10:00 a.m. service. The lush sound of an Esus2 chord echoed from my road-worn Martin dreadnaught, reverberating off of the dilapidated baby blue walls of the elementary school hall in which our small church plant had been meeting since 1999. Before the final chord dissipated and was swallowed whole forever by the creaky floorboards and colonial-style walls, a jarring, boisterous voice contributed a completely unexpected and uninvited element of counterpoint to my momentary spiritual bliss. In a paradigmatic, quintessential Bostonian accent—the ubiquitous timbre and aural texture of which is not unlike that of the cries of an agitated eagle mixed with the grit of the tone of an 82-year-old voice of a chain-smoking nana, fed through an exceedingly trebly megaphone—there bellowed a voice which said unto me, "My Gawd, kid. Stop playin' so many songs that sound so Cathlick." My eyes, still closed up until this point, slowly opened, as my prior state of sublime spiritual basking instantly gave way to a mood now governed by the boiling of my blood spurred on by the catalyst of a classic New England roast. One thought raced to my righteously angry mind: *Steve Jones*.

This was only the most recent installment of Steve's Bostonian-flavored, pre-Sunday-morning-service, chop-busting sessions, the weekly recapitulation of which had been a leitmotif of the past year of church life. Strangely, in New England at least, this form of communication is considered friendly jesting, a paradoxical style of harsh insult hurling, meant as a sort of urban small talk. Steve was a friend, and his frequent friendly fire was almost always reciprocated by an equally insulting response from me after which we both would laugh in unity.

Thus my response up until this point had been, I thought, gracious, patient, and participatory. After all, no one was getting hurt, and a daily dose of a Bostonian roast came with the territory of church planting in the region. Apart from the Holy Spirit, you need at least two things to plant a church in New England: thick skin to survive a jesting roast from a friend and a medium roast from Dunkin' Donuts to provide a sufficiently caffeinated response. Furthermore, the land of Fenway Park, Samuel Adams Brewery, and the Back Bay required a healthy dose of aggression in all domains, particularly the road. Simply by not reciprocating a certain nonverbal communicatory gesture when sharing the road (which to Bostonians is "just being honest"), Christians living and driving in Boston may in fact earn and prove their sanctification.

Yet despite all of the cultural givens, in the case of my reoccurring Sunday morning roasts from Steve, something was starting to happen in my heart. In all honesty, my skin wasn't as thick as I pretended nor was my attitude so seared into the Platonic Bostonian ideal that my feelings were impervious to hurt and harm. On this particular Sunday, after Steve's second dose of insults, my months of accumulated annoyance exploded in a really nasty manner.

"You're playin' so much stuff that's wicked slow," Steve said, following up the friendly penultimate insult with some of his original biblical exegesis. "It says in the Psalms to bang the cymbals, shout for joy, and to sing a new song," at which point he broke out into an impromptu, stunning rendition of "Mighty to Save" to prove his point, complete with Southie Boston accent ("Everyone needs a Save-yah . . . Ah Gawd is mighty to save"). "Come awn," Steve shouted, at this point actually seeming to be somewhat annoyed with me, "follow the Bible on how to lead worship!"

Boom! It was on. "I think I know what the Bible says, Steve," I responded in the most condescending tone that I could invoke. "In fact," I said, following it up with the geekiest verbal punk uppercut I could imagine, "I could recite to you whatever the Bible says about worship and music in the original Greek and Hebrew without a lexicon if it would help you." I finished with a solid final move of arrogance, "Don't presume to teach me about what the Bible says, Steve, and if you want to, then let's step in the ring and see who knows best about how to rightly divide the Word. I'd bet all my chips on myself over you."

Adding fuel to the fire would not be an adequately intense way of describing the subsequent inferno of fury that I instigated and that erupted in Steve in response to my snarky retort. "I knew it!" he said. "You're a lousy hypocrite! You've become a scholarly Bible snob. You think you're so much bettah than everyone else. Seminary big shot!" he shouted. His shocked response culminated with the classic Bostonian altercation crescendo, the one reserved only for situations when someone seriously insults you or your mother (pronounced: muh-tha). "Get over here! Let's go! I want to fight you right heyah right now, kid!"[1]

Oh boy, I thought, *I think I just stepped over the line here.* After being held back by Deacon Dan, Steve calmed down. The two of us went into separate rooms until the service started. Both of us were really upset by the incident, which took place twenty minutes before the service was to begin. The tale ended happily with an ancient Bostonian reuniting ritual which in this case involved talking it out with some frank words outside of the sanctuary, taking communion together, and then going to eat massive cheeseburgers after the service as a kinship (i.e., an "Oh, good, we didn't kill each other") celebration at a local pub.

What happened in this situation that caused the tension to rise to the point of a near-epic ninja ultimate fighting worship festival in the sanctuary of our church? I would venture to say it lies in my adoption of a style of interpersonal interaction that I wrongly assumed to be the "virtue" of passive aggression. Yes, it is true that both Jesus and Paul exhort us to count others as more important than ourselves and thus to set aside our preferences and to bear one another's burdens (e.g., Mk 10:45, Gal 6:2, Phil 2). However, they call us to engage in this behavior neither as silent, impassible stoics nor as wounded, passive-aggressive doormats but as cruciform, cross-bearing truth tellers (e.g., Eph 4:15; cf. Jn 1:17; 8:31-32; 17:17; 1 Cor 5:8; 13:6; 2 Cor 13:8; Phil 1:18; 1 Jn 1:6, 8; 3:18). While my outer self was participating in the brutally honest culture of Bostonia, my inner self was churning in rage, waiting to be unleashed upon whoever had the misfortune of pushing me too far at the wrong time.

The danger here was that I carried out my passive-aggressive response in the name of embodying the ethos of a gentle Jesus. Such Christian stoicism passes itself off as a virtue when it is actually a vice. The act of concealing one's true feelings in favor of a subcultural Christian protocol of politeness is not, in fact, a demonstration of cruciform deference, but is, rather, an act of willful dishonesty. Furthermore, the Greek word *praus*, which is the word used in the Sermon on the Mount to express the concept of meekness and gentleness, refers not (as it is often assumed) to a wimpy, uninvolved celebration of passivity but rather to the concept of "not being overly impressed by a sense of one's self-importance."[2] Therefore, when it comes to the Christian, the call is not to a hippie-esque, aloof indifference but to a rightly ordered and aggressive pursuit of holiness, love, order, and reconciliation on the basis of the power, provision, and greatness of God, and not on the basis of our own pedigree and knowledge. To be meek, as Peter Kreeft has noted, is not to be weak.[3] It is to act in accordance with who we are as servants of the Lord, rather than as lords ourselves. Jesus calls us to relinquish aggression for its own sake, and to aggressively practice the enactment of reconciliation and love.

A Counterculture of Truth-Telling

Holy Scripture beckons us not to the cultivation of politically correct discourse and dishonest communication but instead to its crucifixion so that we can live according to a new narrative of truth-telling. We are called out of the old, decaying culture of deceitfulness into the new creation culture of compassionate, charitable honesty. In the Old Testament, we are exhorted in the Ten Commandments to avoid bearing false witness (Ex 20:16; Deut 5:20). Likewise, those who have "lying lips" (Prov 12:22), who "breathe out lies" (Prov 6:19; cf. 19:5), and who bear "false witness" are uniformly condemned as being abominations who will perish at the hands of the Lord. The violent and rebellious enemies of God and the false prophets are described as liars, not the righteous people of God (Is 30:9; Jer 23:26, Mic 6:12). In the New Testament, lying is routinely rejected, and in fact in Revelation 21:8 liars, along with the cowardly, the faithless, the detestable, the murderers, the sexually immoral, and the sorcerers and idolaters, are the occupants of the lake of fire. Paul himself exhorts the church directly, "Do not lie to one another," in Colossians 3:9.

Yet we continue to promote as a virtue dishonestly withholding truth as a mechanism of avoiding interpersonal conflict in the church. This must stop. We must begin to instantiate and embody the way of the cross in our congregational communication by viewing passive-aggressive behavior as a vice to be eliminated rather than a virtue to be developed. We must create and cultivate a church culture, beginning with the leadership, in which the sin of lying by omission is seen for what it truly is—namely, a grievous, deadly, suffocating, vicious, soul-lacerating, heart-of-Jesus-wounding, dishonest, anti-gospel land mine waiting to destroy the temple of God, the church. Interpersonal relationships in the church ought not to be governed by either the narrative of power and politics or the narrative of passive aggression. Instead, our listening and responding must be governed by patient truth-telling energized by the Holy Spirit, who empowers us to speak the truth in love and thus to be transformed by enacting and receiving cruciform love.

CONCLUSION: CHARTING THE COURSE FOR A STUDY OF INTERPERSONAL CRUCIFORMITY

In the chapters that follow, I am going to address the topic of interpersonal cruciformity within the relationships of the local church. I will approach the topic in two main segments: namely, interpersonal cruciformity between the worship leader and other congregants (including the worship team) and interpersonal cruciformity between the worship leader and other ministry leaders/pastors. Three different narratives or approaches (two negative, and one positive) to interpersonal relationships will be addressed in each section: the narrative of passive aggression (leading as doormats), the narrative of power, coercion, and politics (leading as lords), and the narrative of cruciform love (leading as servants). A brief, preliminary word about each of these approaches to interpersonal relationships in the local church is needed, however, before proceeding.

The narrative of passive aggression (leading as doormats) is the view that mistakes the others-centered, cruciform way of God in Christ for passivity in interpersonal communication and conflict avoidance at all costs. This narrative wrongly associates cruciform love with a noncommittal, sheepish, stoic silence. As we have seen in the opening example, such an approach is not only inconsistent with authentic interpersonal cruciformity, but it is also positively destructive and sinful.

On the completely opposite side of the spectrum is the narrative of power, coercion, and politics (leading as lords). This approach to ecclesial relationships adopts the common, worldly paradigm of the will to power in which effectiveness in leadership and the *pax ecclesia* (the peace of the church) is accomplished through the potency of manipulative maneuvering, aggressive rule, and coercive practices. It is the adoption of the leadership style of Rome rather than that of Jesus. The *pax Romana* (the "peace" of Rome) was achieved through violence, coercion, and force— through the myth of redemptive violence. But Christian leaders bring about the true *pax ecclesia* not by threatening people with the terror of the cross but by walking in the way of the cross in selfless, others-centered, cruciform love. At the cross, the will to power and the myth of redemptive violence died so that the way of the crucified King could bring life, peace, true power, and reconciliation.

The third approach to interpersonal communication and cruciformation in the local church is the narrative of cruciform love (leading as servants). In what follows, I will continue to apply the theology of cruciformational worship to the interpersonal relationships of the church. I will highlight some tangible ways that cruciformational theology can be lived out in practice. Last, I will conclude the section by presenting a positive conversation/case study with my former ministry colaborers. Pastor Walter Kim and Damon Addleman from historic Park Street Church in Boston discuss with me our experience of leadership in the way of the cross, which builds up the church and transforms both ministers and congregants.

INTERPERSONAL CRUCIFORMITY IN THE CONGREGATION

One type of interpersonal cruciformational relationship that occurs in the church is that which takes place between the worship leader and other congregants in the church. This chapter provides some core principles for walking in the way of the cross with our brothers and sisters in the worshiping community. The focus will be on two areas of interpersonal cruciformity—namely, the task of vision casting and that of embracing the absurd in congregational life.

CASTING VISION TO THE CONGREGATION IN THE WAY OF THE CROSS: RELINQUISHING POWER AND AVOIDING POLITICS

For the sake of the health of the body of Christ, worship leaders must lead. "Of course!" one might say. "Leading the congregation in musical worship is integral to the task and responsibility of the worship leader." However, in calling worship leaders to be cruciform leaders, I am not here referring to the musical elements. Leadership in this context refers to courageous and intentional vision casting in regard to the style and spirit of congregational worship. The body of Christ to which we belong and in which we are set apart to serve and lead provides the unique context of this leadership.

Casting vision is not contrary to the cruciform way of God in the congregation, the way that lays down its own preferences for the sake of the other, but instead serves and facilitates the cruciformation of the church. A disregard for discernment and focus in the areas of the ethos, asthetic, and telos—that is, the vibe, style, and goal—of the local congregation's worshiping experience is not humble Christlikeness but embodied, disinterested complacency.

Many worship leaders (myself included) are not naturally comfortable with directive leadership; we much prefer a collaborative group approach. I believe this impulse is good and needed in the church. It guards us from being bossy, creative dictators who operate under the myth of the narrative of power, coercion, and politics. Yet the fact remains that a refusal to lead— and in this case, a refusal to cast vision—creates a vacuum of vision that cries out to be filled. And it will be filled, either by us or by another leader in church, or even by a member of the congregation with a stronger or simply more persistent personality. The pressure resulting from such a detached, doormat mentality masquerading as humility will, as we have seen in my own interaction with Steve Jones, contribute to passive-aggressive patterns of behavior that explode into community destroying instantiations of sin.

I recall a situation that occurred when I was first hired to a new post as the contemporary worship leader in a large, urban church. Almost immediately, a congregant from the church who I'll call Stan began calling me frequently to express how glad he was that I was now in leadership. "Change needs to come to this place," he said. "It is in need of a new, fresh outpouring of God's Spirit through diverse styles of music." After a few calls, though, it became apparent that this man's real interest was in being able to dictate every element of the vision for this new style of worship. To make matters worse, his desire to engage in a more ad hoc improvisational musical style of worship was completely out of step with where I—with the excitement and support of the other pastors in the church—was taking the direction of the musical worship. Further correspondence with Stan by phone and email indicated that he was unwilling to follow the lead and vision of anyone in leadership in the church, including me. He would become observably agitated when asked to abide by the patterns we were trying to set. There came a point in this fiasco at which Stan invited himself to play at the Sunday service, announcing via text, "I'll see you in a few hours for worship." He did this despite my repeated phone and email conversations with him indicating that scheduling for the worship band was done through the online app Planning Center, weeks in advance, and required specific rehearsal commitments, which he had not yet fulfilled.

At that point I had to make a decision: either Stan was calling the shots and casting the vision or I was. I decided, after seeking counsel with my ministry colaborers in the church, that sharp, serious, and strongly worded gospel leadership and admonition was in order lest the situation escalate and disrupt the unity of the congregation. I called Stan and let him know that he would not be playing that evening, but that the following week, I'd be happy to have him on. His response was to leave a phone message followed by an email, indicating that he was withdrawing from the church band. The following is an actual excerpt from my email response to Stan, which both sincerely thanked him for being willing to consider serving at the church by joining the worship band while also sternly rebuking him for his divisive method of communication and lack of willingness to be taught and led:

Dear Stan,

Sorry to hear that you've decided to withdraw from working with us on percussion for the 15th of December and thereafter. I've no doubt concerning your skill, passion, and commitment as a musician and worshiper of Jesus Christ. It is regrettable that you and I seem to disagree on the method of scheduling.

In my defense, I've told you several times—through email, text message, and phone conversation—that there is a strict policy of scheduling for musicians that is followed at our church and that is not conducive to last minute add-ins of any kind. This goes for all our musicians, all of whom are professional players and of the highest quality, yourself included. My apologies that this is disappointing to you, but again, that is not how we schedule at the church. My hope is that you find a church more suitable to your desire to be able to have more spontaneity in that area.

At this church we consider planning and arranging music to be more than an ad hoc affair, and thus a matter of obedience to God.

A great deal of time and care goes into every aspect of the service including the intentional arranging of songs to suit particular musical bands for each service. We won't be changing that. End of story. I consider people just showing up unannounced to be conducive to musical slop and not indicative of intentional, godly planning. As a matter of principle, I don't answer repeated phone calls or texts that disrespect my clear instructions by asking me to change that policy. Is this clear?

Stan, it is clear that this church and you are not a good match. And this is ok! I trust that God will use you elsewhere, perhaps in a place that exercises a more loose musical program, to contribute in meaningful ways to the body of Christ. While it is regrettable whenever the people of God run into roadblocks, it is ok. All I can do is bless you, affirm your gifting, and say to God be the glory wherever you lead. And in so doing, may your joy be complete in Christ Jesus our Lord.

Blessings in Christ Jesus,

John

Was this an example of leading as a lord, exercising coercion and manipulation to further my own agenda? I don't believe it was, and it certainly wasn't my intention to behave under that narrative or power. The composition of the letter above took several hours and went through countless edits in an effort to be intentional about rooting my words in the way of the cross. The experience was bathed in prayer and the letter was written in correspondence with close friends and fellow ministers of the gospel at the church. The type of drama that a situation such as this creates is not something that I enjoy at all. I am generally happy to avoid at all costs such emotion-draining enterprises. The cost in this case, however, would have been abdicating my responsibility to lead the church into an experience of cruciformational worship because of the sinful and stubborn desires of someone whose ideas were proving contrary to such a vision. Thus just as we must be willing to listen, to learn, to be corrected, and to collaborate, so too we must cast vision in the name of the cross, in the way of the cross, by the power the Spirit that raised Jesus from the dead, to the glory of God, and for the sake of the joy and life of the church. If we can speak criticism in ways that love and seek to build up the other, rather than degrading and deconstructing the other, then we can cast vision as cruciform leaders and not as domineering lords or complacent doormats.

When it comes to congregants who are also volunteers in the music ministry and on the worship team, several general principles must be incorporated into the praxis of congregational cruciformity to facilitate and cultivate transformative relationships. I will address these under two subsections: cruciform commitment and cruciform critique. Let's briefly consider these basic precepts and imperatives as we seek to incarnate the gospel to and through the congregants involved in worship.

CRUCIFORM COMMITMENT

Central to a unity-pursuing, Christ-embodying vision and praxis for cruciformational congregational worship is the intentional commitment to commitment itself. Far too often, in the name of what I thought was Christlike deference and being laid back, I allowed volunteer musicians in the congregation to engage in problematic and immature behavior without any critique or consequence. There would be drummers who had been scheduled and had rehearsed for a particular Sunday service who, upon the start of the service, would just not show up and would give no indication that they weren't coming. I had various instrumentalists who came and went without any sort of accountability or expectations. Such leadership is in fact an abrogation of leadership and thus disobedience and cowardice. Nonconfrontational leadership is an ideal soil for the successful planting of passive aggression. I am not advocating a heavy-handed approach to issues related to the unpredictable behavior of volunteer musicians. Rather, the way of the cross cultivates a community ethos among worship team members that views commitment as a thread that weaves the team together. Without the reciprocity of others-centered cruciform commitment, true gospel community cannot exist. We need to resist the temptation to capitulate to the cowardly comfort of complacency or apathy in regard to commitment. Instead, we must embody the way of the cross, intentionally covenanting with one another as a worship team to be resolved to the practice and pursuit of reliable, constant, cruciform commitment as a first principle toward building a creative community of worship arts in the local congregation.

Cruciform Critique

As worship leaders—and really, in any capacity or vocation as human beings created in the image of God—we need to be pursuing a culture of cruciform critique and humble, honest, caring, constructive criticism. Mark Harris, a worship pastor a Gateway Church, captures the ethos and praxis of cruciform critique when he frames it within the context of Christian honesty.[1] To refrain from offering constructive criticism to a member of the worship team is to abdicate responsibility to lead with honesty and integrity. I recall leading in a church during my early twenties in which the pastor and I encouraged the congregants to show up twenty to thirty minutes before the service to sing or contribute to the music with virtually no rehearsal. At the time, I considered this style of leadership to be Christlike and relaxed. However, this hands-off, hippie-style approach led to some really strange and embarrassing situations that, I realize now, were essentially my fault. For example, we had a young, high-school aged girl come to sing who passionately loved music and singing. She would hold her ear in the style of Mariah Carey to ensure that her pitch was perfect. Sadly, the girl is living proof that some people truly are tone-deaf. Not only was she never (and I mean never) even close to being in tune; she was singing in completely different keys, to entirely different rhythms, for one-hundred percent of the time. Yet because I wanted to avoid hurting her feelings, I opted to say nothing. Once again, this was an example of passivity on my part mistaken for cruciformity.

In my own defense, part of my aforementioned doormat mentality that abdicated the responsibility and privilege of true Christian, cruciform critique resulted from an intentional desire to flee from the bossiness and dictatorial tendencies of my earlier years. Before becoming a Christian, it was common practice for me to physically respond to sloppy drumming in my band by executing a flying karate kick of rage into the drum set during the middle of a show. I was known for leading bands as a ruthless tyrant with an iron fist, and this led to nothing but misery for everyone involved.

I thought this was a small price to pay for excellence. However, one can achieve excellence without resorting to either apathetic passivity about atonality or aggressive, kick-drum karate. In between these extremes lies the middle way of cruciformity, which yields a far more satisfying result in terms of both the musical quality and the emotional experience.

To give and receive critique within the context of the worship team, the worship leader must pursue a level of comfortability with directive leadership. Avoiding a musical problem will not fix an issue. Nor will attacking the person responsible for the issue contribute to any sort of resolution and result of excellence. Rather, the worship leader must speak the truth honestly in the manner of love (Eph 4:15). It is cowardly to avoid confrontation but it is courageous and kind to lead your team by engaging in honest, caring, and gentle—but direct and clear—constructive criticism. As the worship leader you are the pedagogue, the guardian, and the overseer of the musical components of worship. Do not forsake this part of your pastoral calling and, on the other hand, do not revel in it as an end in itself. Rather, engage in honest critique for the sake of the cruciformational power of the gospel incarnated in community through psalms, hymns, and spiritual songs.

Expecting, Embracing, and Enjoying Absurdity in Congregational Interpersonal Relationships

The church is a family in Christ full of amazing, annoying, and sometimes absurd relationships. As worship leaders we can approach and react to congregational absurdity in three ways. We can simply ignore the absurd, thereby functioning as doormats, becoming puffed up with passive aggression until we either burn ourselves out from our inner wrath and annoyance or worse, burn someone else when we unleash the furious fire of collected rage. Alternately, we could aggressively annihilate the absurdity by leading as lords, unwilling to accept anything but a perfect and paradisaical church experience in which all things are proper and in their place under our sovereign thumb. Or as I am suggesting here, we could embrace and even enjoy absurd situations and relationships by leading as servants of all people, including the weird, the stranger, and the outcast in the way of the cross as human beings, created equal in the image of God.

I've experienced all of these various reactions to congregational absurdity during my years leading worship in the church, and I have been greatly amused to have myself been the absurd one par excellence. In regard to passive-aggressive approaches to absurdity, I knew a rather large doormat of a fellow, who had the amazing skill of withholding all of his anger and annoyance with congregants and his worship team while at the same time maintaining a smile that said to its viewer: "I'm completely delighted in this moment and I'm glad you are annoying me!" When I observed this worship leader dealing with a delightfully awful drummer who insisted on playing disco-style beats behind almost every very non-disco worship song in the set, I noticed that coupled with his impressive passive-aggressive grin was an intense reddening of the face that looked like my middle-aged balding head after having spent a day under the intense sun of the desert without any sunblock. The man literally resembled a smiley teapot about to explode (set to ecclesial disco music). Dare I say, it was utterly amusing; but also, it was of course detrimental to congregational relationships. As we've been observing, there is no virtue in the lie of omission or the cowardice that we call passive aggression; there is only, we can now say, smiley, sunburnt-teapot syndrome.

Other times I have been the absurd one. This experience reminds me that, yes, I am strange and, more important, I am not above the strange, the weird, the weak, and the outsider. It is so easy to forget as Christians in the church that when we read about Jesus eating with tax collectors and sinners, we are the tax collectors and sinners. Often the question is framed: "How will we be a church who welcomes the outsider, the tax collector, and sinner?" However, the way the question is posed presupposes that we ourselves are something other than the outsider. The moment we forget that we who are already at the table are ourselves sinners being made saints by the grace of God, we forget the gospel. When we come into contact with the odd, the outsider, and the absurd, we must remember that we are not doing this person (who we presume to be below us on account of their strangeness) a favor by putting up with them and letting them hang out with us, as if we were somehow in our "normalcy" (whatever that is!) better than the person. That is not cruciformity; that is superiority, and it is a part of the death-waging sin nature that was nailed to the cross and defeated by our resurrected Lord and Savior. We will never be able to love someone if we think that we are above them. Instead, we need to cultivate a heart for every person in the church and in the world as coequal creatures created in God's image and likeness, whom God is eager to redeem, save, and set free through the gospel of Jesus Christ embodied by his church.

Included on my own congregational oddball résumé and CV are many circumstances and characteristics that demonstrate my requisite sanctified weirdo credentials. Early in my own walk with Jesus, I was perplexed that an older woman in the congregation expressed disgust at my choice of attire, namely, a Social Distortion T-shirt complete with a skeleton smoking a cigarette and drinking alcohol. At that time, I couldn't understand why this woman was "very seriously disturbed" by the shirt I thought was wicked awesome. This particular encounter with the oddball (me) was graciously handled by the woman, and it helped me to be aware that my choice of shirts—including unfortunately my "Keith Richards for President" shirt—could possibly serve to distract people away from the Lord during a time of worship. To me, this was an important lesson, albeit one that led to a much plainer worship attire of plain black T-shirts sans whiskey-slurping skeletons and the partisan politics of one who has sympathy for the devil. There have been probably hundreds (yes, hundreds) of other examples of situations in which I was loved as the outsider, the other, and the oddball.

Sometimes absurdity comes knocking during a worship service in ways that you would never expect and in a manner for which you could never practice, or to which you could never possibly plan a poised response. Take for example the tale of Dennis. Dennis was a random guy who used to attend a Roman Catholic church where I led music for the evening contemporary service circa 2000.[2] In the Roman Catholic tradition, the height of each service is the liturgy of the Eucharist, the Lord's Supper, in which, to the Catholic, the bread and wine become the body, blood, soul, and divinity of Jesus Christ. Even to the person not familiar with Roman Catholic or high church Protestant (e.g., Anglican or Lutheran) liturgy, the holiness and reflective sublime nature of the eucharistic moment is apparent. The minister, invoking the words of Jesus at the Last Supper, holds up the bread and says, "This is my body, broken for you." Next, he takes the cup and says, "This is my blood of the new covenant, which is shed for you and for all for the forgiveness of sins. Drink this in remembrance of me." At this point, a bell rings to indicate the presence of Christ in the elements and the entire congregation sits in silence for a few seconds until the cantor (singer) leads the congregation in the liturgical song, the "Agnus Dei" (Latin for "Lamb of God"). But on this particular occasion—directly after the ringing of the bell, while the priest was still holding up the bread and wine—Dennis, jolted awake from his sermon-induced slumber, proclaimed in a loud, Boston accent, "Dinner time!" Swallowing back laughs that were almost insisting on bursting out, I, the cantor, began to sing the "Agnus Dei":

> Lamb of God, you take away the sin of the world. Have mercy on us.
> Lamb of God, you take away the sin of the world. Have mercy on us.
> Lamb of God, you take away the sin of the world. Grant us peace.

Somehow, we all got through it and continued in worship together, including Dennis, who I'm pretty sure was intoxicated and, apparently, also hungry for dinner. There were other crazy happenings too. Once, a squeamish youth group kid fainted midservice because of our daily theme, the blood of Jesus.

Topping the list of ecclesial absurdities and a close second to Dennis's dinner time was the zany fellow who complimented me after a service for my musical worship and then proceeded to share with me a bizarre story about his own past musical experiences. He said, and I quote, "I used to have a harmonica . . . but then I ate it."

My jumbled response was something like, "Ohhh . . . Ah, wow. I see . . ."

The man continued (and this is literally what he said), "I ate it, and then I $#!+ it out!"

Stunned, I could only respond, "Wow. That's really too bad."

CONCLUSION: INTERPERSONAL CRUCIFORMITY IN THE CONGREGATION

To what verse of Scripture, worship arts primer, seminary course, or program can we turn to prepare us to love and serve the sometimes hysterical, self-proclaimed harmonica-eating, drunk, sick, squeamish, and strange people of God in such unpredictably absurd contexts and predicaments? How can we equip ourselves to be ready for whatever oddities, misfits, and malfunctions the Lord might throw our way? I don't think there is one verse, or even a collection of verses that will assist us to prepare for such situations. Instead, I think the solution is a commitment to the way of the cross, which pours itself out for the other rather than pulverizing the stranger under the hammer of the will to power or passively pretending to put up with the other while simultaneously feeling superior and hateful toward them. Embodying the way of the cross means preparing our souls for congregational catastrophe and ecclesial oddities so that we might react neither by the narrative of superiority nor by the myth of false humility. Rather, we respond by the revolutionary love of the cross, by the power of the resurrection, through the agency and ministry of the Holy Spirit. At the table of God's grace, in the family of the Living God, we need to practice gracious intentionality that isn't threatened by or complacent about the absurd and strange.[3] Instead, we embrace, invite, and even enjoy the challenge of bearing the burdens of the broken, weird, and ridiculous—including the chiefs of all, ourselves.

As the people of God, if we really want to experience the kingdom here and now, we have to cease viewing the church as a table where the squeaky clean, sterilized, and totally sanctified people are doing the inviting and are completely other in quality from the dirty folks they graciously allow to enter the fellowship. Instead, we need to remember that the love that redeems and rescues us tax collectors, sinners, and oddballs calls us to invite more of the same to sit at the table of the free grace of God. While, no doubt, eternal life will exhibit a completely renewed and sanctified human existence, I wouldn't be surprised, based on what the gospels say about Jesus and who he hung out with while walking this earth, if eternity were more absurd than sophisticated.

12

INTERPERSONAL CRUCIFORMITY
WITHIN THE PASTORAL STAFF

T he second domain of interpersonal cruciformity in the church is the area occupied by worship leaders and other vocational ministers and pastoral staff within the congregation. In particular, I've noticed that the relationship between the lead preaching pastor and the worship leader can become an area that is susceptible to a variety of sinful patterns of behavior and communication, from both sides. This is often due to a disconnect in vision between the worship leader and the lead pastor concerning the role and responsibilities of the worship leader. The position of worship leader can be viewed by either the worship leader or the lead pastor as an aesthetic accompaniment to the main event of the sermon, functioning simply as a sort of icing on the cake. Alternately, the position of worship leader can be perceived as a serious vocation and calling of the ministry of the Word through psalms, hymns, and spiritual songs. The problem arises when either party, the worship leader or the lead pastor, has a view of worship leadership that clashes with the understanding of the other person. Oftentimes, the issue is not with an individual's actions but with the underlying vision; clashing of vision in regard to ministry roles frequently contributes the most fuel to the fire of interpersonal friction. Thus it is imperative for both worship leaders and lead pastors to work from the same vision in regard to the roles and responsibilities of the worship leader.

CASTING A VISION OF WORSHIP AND WORSHIP LEADING

The criteria for leadership applied to preaching pastors is not usually applied to worship leaders. This is the root of the majority of interpersonal problems between colaborers in the local church. Rather than being rigorously examined for their theological knowledge and character, worship leaders are often selected primarily on the basis of their musical skill and their fit with the particular congregation in terms of musical style. Adherence to the church's doctrinal statement is also a part of the interview process, but beyond this, the worship leader is generally not held to the same standards of theological training and acumen as the lead preaching pastor. This makes practical sense, though taken to an extreme might result in a charismatic worship leader slaying people in the Spirit during a forty-seven-minute, Hillsong-style music set at a cessationist church that normally only sings hymns—that is, situations that would be highly amusing (subliminal message: make this happen and invite me) but not particularly wise. The New Testament calls worship leaders to a higher standard. The Bible demands from worship leaders the same standard of biblical excellence as that of lead pastors. Furthermore, Scripture places upon worship leaders the same weighty responsibility of the ministry of the Word as that which falls upon the preaching pastor.

In the context of chapter three of Paul's epistle to the Colossians, he writes this profound statement:

> And let the peace of Christ rule in your hearts, to which indeed you were called in one body. And be thankful. Let the word of Christ dwell in you richly, teaching and admonishing one another in all wisdom, by means of singing psalms and hymns and spiritual songs, with thankfulness in your hearts to God. (Col 3:15-16 ESV, though Col 3:16 is my translation)

Likewise in Ephesians 5:18-21, Paul writes this:

> And do not get drunk with wine, for that is debauchery, but be filled with the Spirit, by means of speaking to one another in psalms and hymns and spiritual songs, by means of singing and making melody [lit. "psalming"; Greek *psallontes*] to the Lord with your heart, giving

thanks always and for everything to God the Father in the name of our Lord Jesus Christ, submitting to one another out of reverence for Christ. (Eph 5:18-21 ESV, though Eph 5:19 is my translation)

Most contemporary translations ambiguously render these Greek participles that refer to singing. They are typically translated simply as "singing" with no explanation as to how the participles relate to the main verbs. Based on the grammatical information provided in the Greek, the present adverbial Greek participles translated "singing" indicate not merely that singing is taking place but more specifically, that the singing is the means by which Christ's Word dwells in the hearts of the congregants. Grammatically, singing itself is the instrument by which the tasks of teaching and admonishing—actions usually associated primarily with the preaching of the Word in the sermon and the office of the preaching pastorate—are accomplished in the church!

Likewise, in the passage from Ephesians, Paul exhorts us to be filled with the Spirit. Once again, the means by which the filling with the Spirit occurs in the midst of corporate worship is through song. Grammarians of the Greek New Testament refer to these grammatical elements as the dative of instrument (in reference to the nouns *psalms*, *hymns*, and *songs* in Colossians) and, in regard to the participial forms, adverbial participles of means or instrument. In plain English, the grammatical terms for singing express that partaking in song during worship is the means by which the main verbs (*teaching, admonishing,* and Spirit/Word *indwelling*) are accomplished. This is hugely significant for articulating a vision for the role and responsibilities of the worship leader in the local church.

On the basis of this theological precept, we must say that the person tasked with choosing, leading, and engaging the congregation with the musical components of the worship service is, in fact, not merely a wind-up worship music monkey, an artsy, skinny-jeans-wearing, cool-beard-like-David-Crowder, Rivers-Cuomo-awesome-emo-glasses-wearing, Starbucks-fiending, listens-to-Sufjan-Stevens-and-some-obscure-indie-alt-country-bands non-heretic. No! According to the New Testament, worship leaders are tasked with helping us to do at least three things. Worship leaders are meant to do the following:

- Worship leaders minister the word of Christ to us so that it can dwell in us through psalms, hymns, and spiritual songs.

- Worship leaders assist us through music in teaching and admonishing one another in the gospel Word and the gospel call to Christlike transformation as a community, the body of Christ.

- Worship leaders help us experience the ministry and presence of the Holy Spirit precisely through psalms, hymns, and spiritual songs.

Thus I must offer the following exhortation to both worship leaders and lead pastors:

If you are a worship leader, you are more than just a tag-along to sing Jesus songs which complement the theme of the sermon; you are a minister of the inspired, infallible Word of God and the gospel of Jesus Christ. Are you prepared and/or preparing yourself for this weighty task? Consider the call and proceed wisely.

If you are preaching pastor, your role is integral to the gospel fellowship of the church, but the ministry of the Word is not constrained to the preaching or the pulpit. Rather, it etches itself into the souls of the saints through the transformative Word of Christ as it dwells in the hearts of the faithful by the mode of musical worship and liturgy.

A good deal of interpersonal ministerial strife is created when either party—the worship leader or the lead pastor—oversteps the bounds of their own role into the role of the other. It most frequently happens from the direction of the lead pastor toward the worship leader. Nobody enjoys being micromanaged, but it happens all the time, usually inadvertently, when lead pastors overinstruct or even dictate musical selections, style, and vision to worship leaders rather than delegating to them the responsibility to determine these things. Lead pastors are rarely aware that such intrusions are received by the worship leader not merely as inappropriate boundary crossings but as soul-killing exercises that undermine the call and responsibility of the worship leader. When a lead pastor is overly nit-picky, needlessly critical, or generally overbearing in a type-A kind of way, this behavior itself sucks the creative life out of the experience of worship for the worship leader. The result is that from the perspective of the artistic theologian (i.e., worship leader), worship becomes a soulless shell that has been stripped of its inner essence, sensitivity, and power. Leading worship in such a setting is about as fun and creative for a worship leader as playing a grueling three-hour, Top 40 cover gig at a dive bar called Larry's Lounge and Lobster Shack managed by a cruel and vicious lady named Darlene who has forty-seven cats and a tattoo of a demonic-looking pony and a rifle on her left arm—on a Tuesday night for $25, two drink tickets, and a complimentary sloppy lobster dinner. Such a gig has its place in the life experience of a starving artist but it is hardly life-giving. Rather, it is a product of necessity (and perhaps the result of a general love for the consumption of crustaceans).

But how can worship leaders communicate this dissatisfaction with being micromanaged in helpful ways to the lead pastor, with a view toward changing the vision and increasing the expectations of the worship leader as an aesthetic, harmonic, and melodic minister of the Word? I would advise you to consider the following action items as you lead and cast vision about worship in the local church.

First, recast the vision for worship leaders as ministers of the Word. This theological principle must be stated rather than assumed. As I argued above, most worship leaders and church pastors do not view worship leading as a ministry of the Word. Thus we must recast the vision, live into the vision, and thereby bless the church through a reformation of the worship leader's role and responsibility from the "staff position" of a mere musical accompanist to the vocation of a minister of the Word.

Also, adopt the posture of patience and the pattern of the cross as you engage in the ministry of worship. Many churches need to revise their vision for the role of worship leader as more than a wind-up, Holy Spirit music maker. Be patient. Be loving. Be warm and generous. Live into the role and responsibility even if your colleagues aren't completely acknowledging the weight and extent of the role yet. Assist your colaborers and congregants in growing and understanding the theological and vocational seriousness of the role by leading as a minister, even if you're only viewed by the majority of the congregation as a mere musician. In most cases, what will happen is that the pastoral staff will begin to interact with you as a ministry equal, not so much because you articulated a vision in words but because you lived it into reality in the context of a people, walking in the way of the cross.

In denominations or church bodies that practice ordination, pursue ordained ministry. During my time at Park Street Church, most of the congregation had no idea that I was an ordained evangelical Anglican minister with an MDiv and a PhD in theology. However, both my ministry colleagues and I viewed my role as a worship leader in the church as a ministry of the Word. In addition to this, or in place of it (for example, in churches that don't practice ordination), I would encourage you to pursue opportunities to preach in your local congregation if you have this gift and ability. At my current church I preach once per month and lead worship each Sunday. This reminds the congregation (and me) that my service as a worship leader is a form of pastoring and ministering the gospel through music and lyrics.

If you find yourself in a position in which the pattern of interpersonal communication between yourself and the lead pastor(s) is frequent and seemingly unchangeable, you should devote a time of prayerful, communal discernment to the question of whether God may be calling you to a new season of ministry somewhere else. There is no shame in honest, open, collegial, and cruciform conversation with your colleagues and co-laborers in ministry. You should avoid passive aggression and lording leadership at all costs, but the pursuit of open communication in the way of the cross can lead only to growth in Christ rather than fraction and fragmentation. Even if a season of discernment leads all parties to conclude that a new call into a new community is the will of God for you, this process, conducted in a cruciform manner, will itself be the means by which people of contrary and incompatible personalities will themselves be transformed into the image of Jesus. Conversation and discernment in community promotes unity rather than threatening it.

Expecting, Embracing, and Enjoying Absurdity in Congregational Interpersonal Relationships

As was the case with interpersonal relationships within the congregation and within the worship team, absurdity seems to sprout forth from the fertile ground of weirdness that the gospel invites into one community.

The key—as has been the running theme—is avoiding, on the one hand, the doormat, passive-aggressive pattern of life that attempts to ignore the oddities of local church ministry and, on the other hand, resisting the temptation to bark orders at others in order to institute a domineering vision in the church.

Commonly, the instantiation of pastoral absurdity takes place from the direction of preaching pastors toward worship leaders. It is a frequent occurrence for me to, in the context of a conversation with other worship leaders, have a laugh over the strange things requested by those under whom and with whom we serve as co-ministers of the gospel. I've heard stories from my worship leader friends from all over the world about things like their lead pastors' insistence that an obscure, secular, hideously corny, '80s rock tune be included in the liturgy to match a sermon theme, or that a ballet performance be included in the middle of a sermon. Such things are odd. Extremely, utterly, totally, and gloriously odd. Likewise, I remember a lead pastor who was very excited and hopeful that I would incorporate a saxophone into worship. For the particular congregation, any kind of woodwind or brass would have been totally off base. Yet this man was just dying to have someone rip out a soaring Holy Spirit sax solo in the middle of our set. Such a thing is weird. Extremely, utterly, totally, and gloriously weird. At another more charismatic church, I watched the worship leader/preacher deal with a man who was enjoying blowing on his shofar way too much. The worship leader just kept saying: "Thank you, Francis. Thank you, FRANCIS. Thaaaaaank you, Francisssss!" while gesturing with his hand to Francis to wrap up the fanatical horn-blowing festivities. Such behavior is as goofy as it is gloriously absurd.

Other times, the absurdity is the result of our own behavior as worship leaders. I think of the times that I incarnated absurdity in my choices for worship music. Reflecting back, the high-tempo ska version of the typically slow and reflective hymn "The Prayer of St. Francis" likely wasn't a tasteful choice. Watching the minister scurry down the aisle during a processional reminiscent of a Reel Big Fish concert made me rethink the wisdom in that arrangement. Similarly, my Ramones-style rendition of the classic Christmas carol "Hark! The Herald Angels Sing" circa 2002, judging by the faces of the congregation, wasn't quite what people were expecting. (Although, in that case, I believe the absurdity was, in fact, redemptive, beneficial, and justified. After all, I'm quite certain that Jesus himself can be shown to be a fan of the Ramones. I believe evidence of this sure fact can be found somewhere in 1 Corinthians, or at the very least, through a study of natural law which testifies to the general awesomeness of classic punk rock as a universal truth.) In the midst of an imperfect community in process and progress toward perfection through the instantiation of divine love, absurdity can surely be annoying, but through embodying the burden-bearing pattern of cruciformation, it can become an interpersonal means of grace.

A Case Study in Interpersonal Cruciformity at Park Street Church

One of the most profound ministry experiences of my life thus far took place in 2013 and 2014, when I had the privilege of serving as the worship leader for the contemporary evening service at historic Park Street Church in Boston, Massachusetts. I was fresh off the heels of a three-year stint of intense research toward a doctorate in New Testament at the University of St. Andrews in Scotland. My doctoral work, some of which is summarized and applied to the topic of communal worship in this book, focused on the way in which, in the New Testament, the church and the people of God are the means by which renewal takes place—through love, into the image of the God who is love. I spent three years studying this topic deeply, comparing it to Greco-Roman sources, praying about it, and dreaming about it, but I had not yet actually experienced it until coming to Park Street Church. The fear in the back of my mind as I finished my PhD was that perhaps the richness of the theology about which I was writing did not exist in reality. What if my beloved theology of the church couldn't be put into practice because it existed only as an abstract formulation in my mind, unable to be incarnated or experienced in real life, in flesh and blood community?

These fears were quelled not long after my time serving at Park Street began. Far from being a perfect community, my ministry colaborers and I struggled with many things in the urban, imperfect, place that is Boston and Park Street Church. For me to cast any church as perfect would be an exercise in idealization and overly optimistic delusion. Yet in some ways, what was perfect about Park Street to me was not that it was functioning perfectly in every way (it wasn't), but that its perfection (if you will) was in its own awareness as a body and as a ministerial staff that it was, in fact, not at all perfect. This group realization of our corporate and individual imperfection in the midst of our walking together as a community of equals in the way of the cross itself paradoxically provided the way to what the New Testament refers to as growth in perfection—namely, transformation through cruciform love into the perfect image of the God who is love. Only when colleagues and colaborers in ministry are viewed as valuable and worthy of divine, gospel, cruciform love—not on the basis of their résumés, degrees, or worldly accolades but on the basis of their being, as people created in the image of God who now belong to Christ—only then can the collaborative, restorative, renewing grace of God reciprocally heal brokenness, sin, and selfishness through one another in the context of the body of Christ, the church.

Through working with pastor Walter Kim and worship coordinator Damon Addleman, at Park Street I began to realize the most exciting aspect yet to my doctoral work on transformative cruciform love in the church. The theological idea was true, but not because I wanted it to be or because I could prove it through some explication of a Greek participial clause in the New Testament (though, incidentally, I propose that I can). No, it was not true because of participles or abstract theological paradigms; it was true because I was experiencing it in and through relationships with actual people. For the first time in my life, in a holistic, real sense, the church became not a liability, chore, or a stumbling block but rather a privilege, family, and foundation. Here was a place of forgiveness, a family of grace, a foundation of truth, a temple of the Spirit, a body; and I was (and am) a part of it. Of course, this reality is not present only within the Park Street community. It is and can be alive and active wherever the people of God gather together to faithfully receive Word, sacrament, and fellowship by the power of the Holy Spirit, in union with the living God and in communion with the saints across the globe and through the ages.

Thus—on account of my experience of authenticating faith through newly encountering the love and grace of Jesus through his body, and particularly through my time working with my brothers and sisters at Park Street Church—I decided the best way to make this theology of cruciformation practical at the level of ministerial interpersonal relationships would be to have a brief conversation with my colaborers in the ministry at Park Street. The goal is not to offer an ideal or paradigm but simply to present a story of the good, refreshing, true grace of God we got to share and are now still sharing together and with others because of God's loving-kindness to us through this experience as the church. My prayer is that each of you might experience and encounter Jesus anew as his love is incarnated and embodied through real people in profound ways. I pray that you believe more and more that the gospel you know about in your mind is true in your experience and overflows from your heart with joy, into gratitude and an insatiable, unending hope.

John: I think one of the things I appreciated most about ministering and worshiping with you guys was that I felt like the shared leadership experience provided an opportunity both to speak vision and to listen and incorporate the vision and critique of others. When we had our weekly prayer and planning meetings, whether through Skype or in person at the church, I felt that this created a space and a setting for the Spirit to teach us how to lead in the way of the cross, not as domineering lords or dictators, not as passive-aggressive doormats, but as vulnerable, real, and teachable disciples of Jesus. I was so glad and refreshed by the experience of the giving and receiving of criticism not for the sake of furthering one's own agenda or for the protection of one's own ego. It was part of a journey together with Jesus in community, for the sake of the community, and for the glory of God and our joy together in him. On account of this openness, I felt an almost natural ability to peacefully change course at various points in my own vision for elements of the worship ministry based on the good, thoughtfully communicated ideas and observations that were shared in the context of a gospel community of reciprocal grace.

I wonder if you guys might comment on how intentionally pursuing authentic cruciform community blessed and continues to bless you, perhaps commenting on our time as a leadership team. If you could, specifically note what variables in our working relationship made us able to lead with courage and conviction but to do so in the way of the cross rather than according to the narratives of power or passive aggression. Of course we didn't perfectly accomplish this. However, we did, I think, to a large extent find a great peace, satisfaction, and an authenticating experience of the truth of the gospel in it. If you could share a bit on that, it would be great.

Walter: The invitation to collaborate, even after our formal connections have ended, bears witness to the kind of trusting relationship that was so vital and so satisfying to our service together. I found in our team that we not only ministered to a community of congregants but also ministered as a community of leaders. We led as a community to a community. Of course, since I am not a musician, a team approach to leadership was a basic requirement. I needed to trust that Damon, you, and the band were going to pray, prepare, and lead music as a central aspect of our congregation's worshiping life. However, my recognition that ministry requires teamwork is based upon something far more fundamental and significant than the realization that I am not a musician. It involves a fundamental conviction that no one person, however broadly gifted, is the sole repository of grace and truth. Sometimes saying "I need you" is really hard for independently minded Americans because that entails vulnerability. This is, of course, a central lesson of the cross. We are in desperate, profound need.

Consequently, the way of the cross is also a way of humility. John, I greatly appreciated how you invited us to worship God and not just directed us to worship God. You yourself were worshiping and, in so doing, were inviting us to participate with you. This is a subtle but significant difference. There is a fine line between seeking worship that wows versus seeking worship that wows people with God. It is gratifying when someone leaves a service and enthusiastically exclaims, "That was awesome worship!" But it is even more gratifying to hear a person exclaim, "What an awesome God we worship!" The way of the cross deflects attention. This is the way that compelled John the Baptist to say, "He must increase, but I must decrease" (Jn 3:30), or the Son of God not to consider equality with God as something to be grasped (Phil 2:6). I sensed in both you and Damon the use of creativity to bless others rather than to impress them. This held true in our interactions. I never felt that you were trying to impress me, nor in turn did I feel forced into proving myself to you.

Damon: Walter, the texts from John 3 and Philippians 2 you just mentioned, I also think, collectively render the exact lens through which a team of leaders must view their relationship—both to each other, as a smaller group of leaders, as well as to the whole congregation which they lead in music, preaching, etc., during a given service. When working as a leadership team, "a community for the community" of Christ, as Walter put it, there are two hands to balance. On the first hand, a prayed-over, personal vision being expressed, lobbied for, and carried through, and on the other hand, the ultimate mandate of self-sacrifice as ultimately exemplified by Christ. This balance is tricky and perhaps should not be a perfectly even one, because when we have to err toward one hand it has to be to follow the example of Christ. Of course, in order to be effective leaders, God wants us to use the creativity and skills he has entrusted to us to lead his people with conviction and confidence, but not at the cost of self-mutilation. The church body can suffer personal and collective wounds at the "first hand" of our selfish ambitions—no matter how conscious or unconscious we are of it. It is when we err toward this first hand that we risk damaging our relationship and effectiveness with other members of the body and the body as a whole. When following the "second hand" of humility, we never risk matching the example of Christ and this, in a way, makes it easier. Our "sacrifice" is acutely put into perspective against his sacrifice.

It has been my experience working with the two of you that you both deeply understand this and aim to remember it regularly, and I think, in a general sense, that this fact was what made our group dynamic such a positive one. Beyond our leadership group, the challenge with bringing and carrying out an artistic/aesthetic vision for the music or any other aspect of our services is an even greater one, because we have to take into account the needs and desires of the individual members, not to mention the desires and plans God has for that particular body of believers.

John: Now that we've talked generally about cultivating a community of gracious intentionality and cruciform leadership, I'd like to speak specifically about some events and elements that stood out to me. These reminded me that the gospel is true and real and alive in and through the body of Christ, the church. I recall that Tara (my wife) and I felt really blessed to have been invited into Walter and Toni's home after being prayerfully selected to take up the worship leader position at Park Street. There was something about beginning a ministry in the home of a new friend over a meal with other new friends that stuck with me as being a means and marker of grace throughout my time at Park Street. It established a pattern of authenticity and simplicity that helped me to appreciate you guys as people, apart from your roles in the church. There was not a churchiness to the proceedings that evening but the gathering established an unassuming, honest openness that made colaboring in ministry with you guys more like a family affair than a professional, ecclesial post separated from the sort of personal commitment typically required and expected of a real family. Thanks for that grace. Ministry with you guys didn't feel like religion, it felt real; and that was refreshing.

Another occasion came to mind that highlights why our season of ministry together was special and life-giving rather than spiritually and emotionally draining. On our Monday meeting together after a normal Sunday evening service, I remember Walter commented that my style of improvising for long periods of time and deviating from the lyrics on the screen might be confusing to some of the congregants who didn't quite know how to follow me in this form of spontaneity. We then talked about how we could include blank slides in the slideshow for the operator to use as placeholders during these improvisational moments. Further, it was suggested that it might be helpful for me to coach or guide the congregation in a natural manner about precisely what I was doing in these moments, since the style of worship was not something that most folks were used to at Park Street. I remember thinking that because of the ethos we established in our leadership community, and because of the respect I had for your opinions, I did not take this critique as a personal insult at all. Rather, I was truly able to receive it as a helpful tool. There would be many other analogous examples in which I probably offered constructive criticism to you, seeking to do so in a cruciform way. My recollection is that, generally speaking, we engaged in this type of communication quite frequently. I don't remember ever feeling judged, hurt, dictated to, or demeaned. I also got the sense that there were probably smaller critiques any of us could have made but that we deemed matters of personal preference. These critiques remained unvoiced not because of passive aggression. Judging by the patterns of community we set, we decided it wise not to raise them because they did not show themselves to be issues of great importance for the good of the community. They were, in other words, peripheral and nonessential individual preferences. I felt that by not raising every little nitpicky comment and by being able to distinguish between necessary and incidental critique, we were able to encounter the love of God through our critiques, not instead of them. I'm interested to hear your reflections and thoughts on these elements of ministry together.

Walter: As I reflect upon our interactions, two fundamental dispositions come to mind. First, I think that we had the firm belief that we needed to be disciples and not just make disciples. We were all in the process of growing in Christlikeness, and therefore our interactions were as much opportunities to learn and grow as they were responsibilities to help others learn and grow. It really seemed that each of us recognized and acknowledged our own need for development. We also saw the other person's eagerness for growth. So in such an environment, critiques are not given and received as a diminishment but as a commitment to growth and a discovery of something else about God or ministry. This is not so much a commitment to excellence as it is a reflection of discipleship.

Second, coupled to this basic orientation toward learning is also a sense of wonder. Along with most other people, I am amazed by the wonders of creation, whether standing at the edge of the Grand Canyon or staring at a night sky ablaze with the starry host. But more amazing to me is witnessing a person who is filled with the Spirit and serving God. This is a wonder both natural and supernatural, a wonder of creation and re-creation in Christ. The use of natural musical gifts in the power of the Spirit is a cause of great wonder for me because I'm most definitely not gifted that way. There is an openness to be surprised by God's grace when we have this sense of wonder. I recall one worship service when we sang a version of "How Great Thou Art" so arresting, so filled with a sense of divine wonder that I could not preach the sermon as I had prepared it. So I scrapped my carefully crafted introduction so that we could extend this sense of wonder in the worship service. This was a very important reminder for me that the main thing is worship and that I needed to be prepared to bend my will toward that end. If so, I become open to surprising lessons that may come from all sorts of place, including critique or inspiration from colleagues.

These observations connect back to my comments about the cross as a way of humility. When a critique is freed from personal ambition or the need to impress another person or the need to establish a pecking order, it can be given in love and received in love. When there is a sense of wonder at the gifts that God distributes among his people, there is an openness to learn. Such a place of grace enables us to admit our own needs without shame and to trust in another person without guilt.

Damon: As we met to plan and pray, we were able to present our ideas and our critiques to each other's ideas and styles of leading, keeping a firm grasp on the community-serving ideals we'd been talking about and a loose grasp on our own inclinations. When following Christ's example, it makes it much easier to hold loosely, just as he did (Phil 2 again). The necessity of humility to the success of unity cannot be overstated. The need for prayer can never be satisfied. I appreciated that we always took time to start and end our meetings with prayer—for the decisions we faced, both big and small, and for each other's families and personal needs. Those prayers for each other were a balm for any scraped agendas and bruised egos that may have occurred in any discussions, even though we may not have even deemed it helpful to voice them.

I would be remiss to not mention how the hiring of you, John, into the worship leader role was, although a general background aspect of this conversation, a quite specific example of how I personally was challenged to live out this idea of cruciformity. Previous to your arrival, I was generally working in that role or at least saw that the need was met on a weekly basis. Through a series of conversations among church leadership, it was decided that there was a need to change my role to concentrate on other emphases to increase the effectiveness and scope of the evening service and that we would hire someone new to focus on leading the music within the services. Although my new role had engaging challenges for me to focus on, it was tempting to—and could have been easy to—feel insecure, possessive, and even spiteful about releasing my grasp on my previous role, which was still greatly overlapping with my new one. However, although I may have had temporary lapses into such negativity, this was not the general rule. Upon first meeting you and through our ongoing meetings, because of the mindset we've mentioned being firmly held by you and Walter, I was more easily able to loosen my grasp and avoid those temptations. There was a lack of selfish ambition in the midst of striving toward a vision, a lack of establishing a pecking order, to be critical, at least in any sort of reckless way. In contrast, there was the wonder that Walter mentioned in watching your set of gifts being used by God to bless his church in a new, refreshing way, and the shared goal of leading our community in humility and with grace. Having the example set by Christ and the present work being done with colaborers who are like-minded provided a means for me to be open and flexible during that transition and inspired genuine excitement about what he might do through our unity.

John: Thanks, guys. What a privilege and joy it is to have you as brothers in Christ and friends in ministry. I'll close by offering this blessing from 2 Corinthians 13:14 for us and for those reading: "The grace of the Lord Jesus Christ and the love of God and the fellowship of the Holy Spirit be with you all." Amen.

PART 5

CRUCIFORM LITURGY

13

THE LITURGY OF CRUCIFORM WORSHIP

Cruciformation Through Liturgical Ideation

The goal of this chapter is to do one thing, and one thing only: to apply the theology of cruciformational worship to our actions as the people of God at worship through liturgy. The word *liturgy* is one that is sometimes associated with the smells and bells of high church worship such as that found in many Anglican, Lutheran, Catholic, and Orthodox churches. However, in using the word *liturgy* here I am not referring to any particular style of worship, whether high church or low church, but rather as a less cumbersome synonym for the "order of service."

In this sense, every church has a liturgy, an order of events that comprise the worship service. In my thirty-four years of life as a worshiper I have worshiped in a number of different churches that varied in liturgical style and order. As a young child up through my high school years I was raised in the Roman Catholic Church, partaking in a contemporary form of the Catholic liturgical Great Tradition which had its most recent roots in the liturgical reforms and revisions of Vatican II. Then as a twenty-something I worshiped in a Reformed, Baptistic, nondenominational, emerging-style church. During my doctoral years in Scotland, I worshiped in the Scottish Episcopal Church and then in the Free Church of

Scotland. Upon returning to the United States, I became the worship leader at Park Street Church, a historic congregational church in downtown Boston. I am now an Anglican priest worshiping in a moderate low-church style characterized by a mix of evangelical, charismatic, and Catholic streams of spirituality all guided by the liturgical order and riches of the *Book of Common Prayer.*

Your own liturgical journeys may be similarly diverse or they might be much more consistently rooted in one order and style of worship. Perhaps you are on a journey of discovery in terms of denominations and liturgical worship styles as you read this chapter. Wherever you are on your liturgical journey, I want to invite you to consider how the theology of cruciformational worship applies to four major elements of worship that are present (in whatever order or frequency) in all of our traditions: namely, prayer, preaching, sacrament, and song.

While a chapter on liturgy could accomplish a number of objectives—such as considering which liturgical order and style is most conducive to transformative worship, discussing the "how-to" of preaching or prayer as a form of practical theology, or analyzing the theological content of the hymns we sing—we will do virtually none of those things here. Instead, we will focus on the theme of how the Word of God, the Holy Scriptures, makes present the Word of God, Jesus Christ. In other words, through the liturgical actions of prayer, preaching, sacrament, and song, we communally encounter Jesus through the enactment and reception of his love in the life and worship of the body of Christ. In so doing, we will shed more light on how the church—through the experience of love toward the other and from the other—is transformed into the image of the God who is love through his liturgical presence. This process of love made present through Christ in his body will be referred to as "the ecclesio-pneumatic ideation of Jesus Christ."

LITURGICAL IDEATION AS A CATALYST
FOR CRUCIFORMATION

In chapter two we discovered a Pauline pattern of cruciformation in which the singing of psalms, hymns, and spiritual songs plays a major role. The underlying ethos of Paul's understanding of transformative, cruciformational worship is that through walking in the way of God and worshiping with the people of God we are renewed in the image of God. Our characters are formed in accord with the love of Christ through Christ's community of love, the church. This results in a spiritual transformation of the community in the way of the cross—cruciformation. The knowledge of God, it was argued, is not doctrinal knowledge but rather a knowledge of who God is in Christ, which is made present in the ecclesial community by our communal walking in accordance with his will and Word. The perfection of believers in and as the church is the goal of this cruciformational process. It is precisely through the reciprocity of grace and love that we are renewed by the knowledge of the God who is love.

How can we move this theology of cruciformation from the realm of abstract ideas to the realm of concrete ecclesial practices and activities? Or in other words, how is the transformative knowledge of, experience of, and encounter with Jesus Christ made present through the act of communal cruciform worship? The depth and degree of answers to this question are as varied and complex as the totality of Christian theologies about the Holy Spirit, the presence of God in the church, and the power of God in the sanctification of the believer. In a real sense, God's presence with and in us is a mystery, and so too is his transformation of us through this presence. The fullness of the infinite ways and workings of God's incarnational presence will never be mined, transcending both the constraints of human finite cognition and the limited capabilities of language. Recognizing the vastness of the ineffable mystery of God and his presence with us can lead us to only one response: worship.

Yet the task of theology—through an engagement with Holy Scripture, coupled with the illumination and empowering of the Holy Spirit, and knit together through the available philosophical resources at our disposal—endeavors to articulate (albeit imperfectly) a faith that seeks understanding. In so doing, those engaged in the task of theology recognize that the end result of the quest is never mere facts about God but rather the knowledge of God himself. Thus any truth we uncover in the process of seeking to say things about God is not so much about filling an encyclopedia with ideas about God but instead about mediating an encounter with God. It is, to use the title of Brunner's book on revelation, about *Truth as Encounter* rather than truth as information.[1] In the case of the theological question at issue here—namely, the means by which God is present through the people of God in order to transform us through worship—even this theological category could be approached from a variety of theological positions. Thus it is important to note that the theological constructions offered here do not claim to be the one and only way of describing God's presence. Rather, the idea of renewal in the knowledge of the God who is love, through love in communal worship by an ecclesio-pneumatic ideation of Jesus Christ, is one of many ways in which believers participate in the very life of God and are thereby transformed.

THE ECCLESIO-PNEUMATIC IDEATION OF JESUS CHRIST

Having established the starting points for a discussion about the mode and mechanism of the communal experience of Jesus in worship, I must define the odd little phrase "the ecclesio-pneumatic ideation of Jesus Christ." (The first thing to note is that it sounds awesome. Whether or not you will find the idea to be radically illuminating and the best thing since sliced bread, or totally bogus and devoid of all worth, one thing is indisputable: it is a great thing to bring up at dinner parties. By using big theological terms, people will think you are smarter than you really are, and they will have no idea how to argue against what you're saying because they will have no idea what it is that you are actually saying. Other words that fit this bill are *hermeneutics, perichoresis,* and *existential.*) You may be wondering where a dense phrase like "the ecclesio-pneumatic ideation of Jesus Christ" comes from and why I couldn't have chosen an easier, more entry-level concept. While undoubtedly my own creation, I wished to incorporate Wolfgang Iser's insightful work on ideation in reader-response hermeneutics (i.e., interpretation) to the realm of liturgical formation.

So what does the phrase "the ecclesio-pneumatic ideation of Jesus Christ" mean? First, by *ecclesio,* I am referring to the fact that the transformational encounter and presence of Jesus Christ in worship is inherently and inseparably tied to the *ecclesia,* the church. I do not mean to suggest that Christ cannot be encountered individually. However, a permanent divorce of the individual from the church to pursue a purely individual personal relationship with Jesus is not envisioned or taught by any of the apostles or by Jesus himself. The metaphors used by the New Testament authors about the knowledge of God, growth in sanctification and Christian perfection, and the enactment and reception of cruciform love all revolve around the theme of individuals being incorporated into a new collective singular such as a body and a temple. As a result, it is not an overstatement to say that growth in Christian character, sanctification, and the pursuit of transformative encounters with God are at a detriment when pursued on purely individualistic grounds.

Second, in using the transliteration of the Greek word *pneuma*, I am highlighting that the transformative encounter with Christ experienced ecclesially through the embodiment of divine love is never a merely human activity. Rather, it is one that is only possible through the presence and empowerment of the Holy Spirit. In Colossians 1:9, the reader will recall, the Spirit provides the spiritual wisdom and understanding that leads to a knowledge of God's will. Consequently, we engage in communal life and worship that lead us to the knowledge of who God is in himself. Likewise, in Colossians 3:16 the word about Christ dwells in the church precisely through psalms, hymns, and spiritual songs. The Greek adjective *pneumatikais* is not meant to indicate a genre of song in this verse, that is, spiritual as opposed to secular. Rather, the adjective *spiritual* modifies the noun *songs* by describing the empowering force that works through the singing to make present the word about Christ, by which we encounter him and his love through the melody and harmony we create.

Last, the word *ideation* must be defined before applying this paradigm of the transformative ecclesial presence of Christ to a theology of cruciformational worship. In using the concept of ideation to discuss the means by which Christ is present in cruciformational liturgy, I am drawing from the work of Wolfgang Iser and primarily from his 1980 book titled *The Acts of Reading: A Theory of Aesthetic Response*.[2] Iser was a German literary scholar who worked and taught mainly in the area of reader-response hermeneutics known as aesthetic theory. Though Iser's theory is hugely beneficial for the study of theology, he himself was not a theologian and did not apply his work to the discipline of theology or biblical studies. Instead, he wrote almost exclusively about the relationship between text and reader by exploring what happens from the reader's perspective in the act of reading works of fiction. In the most fundamental sense, ideation and aesthetic response (according to Iser) refer to the process in which, when reading a work of fiction, the reader activates the structures and elements of a text that create meaning and in so doing produces an experience through which the characters and world of the text become present.[3] This statement suffices as a summary of Iser's view of ideation. However, parsing out the theory in greater detail before applying it to the process of cruciformational worship will help explain more fully how it works.

TEXT AS A MEANS OF ENCOUNTERING A PERSON: THE BASICS OF ISER'S THEORY OF IDEATION

The theory of aesthetic response in Iser begins with the structures and signs of a text. These structures and signs are not simply the individual words of a text, but rather are a reference to the authorial structuring of the words and phrases in order to communicate ideas. The structures and signs in the literature comprise a "pattern" which "guide[s] the imagination of the reader" to ultimately construct the meaning of a text.[4] And the meaning of a text, for Iser, is never simply a series of propositional facts that are delivered via the text from the author to the reader but is instead an experience.[5] The meaning of a text is not mere information, but the entrance into a "dynamic happening" and a "living event."[6] Through the ideation process, the reader does not simply receive but instead plays a part in constructing the reality brought about by the text. Contrary to the way in which, for example, we would read instructions for the assembly of a piece of furniture or a bicycle, or a recipe for macaroni salad, reading literature requires that the reader participate in the act by forming meaning rather than by simply being passively informed by a list of propositions.[7]

This process of actively forming meaning by following the patterns inherent in a text is the heart of ideation. In the act of reading, the reader "assemble(s) the meaning toward which the perspectives of the text have guided him."[8] Ideation is distinct from other, nonliterary acts of perception in that the entire function of the imagination in the act of reading requires that the object being imagined or ideated be absent, or in the case of fiction, nonexistent. Conversely, nonideational perception outside of the literary realm (e.g., observing a sunset, having a conversation) requires the presence of the object for perception to occur.[9] Thus in the reading of literature, the ideation—the assembly of meaning of a text from the structures in the text—involves an act of endowing presence to something that, apart from the activation of the text by the reader, is in some sense absent. Accordingly, it follows that only in the act of ideation through reading do the words of the page begin to actually mean something. Until reading commences, the words lie dormant in the pages of the book awaiting their activation and ideation.

For the reader, there at least two benefits to understanding the process of ideation: namely, (1) the ability to view the "real" world from the world of the text which we inhabit by ideation and (2) the ability to encounter a character or person who is not accessible to us outside of the text. Let's briefly say a word about both of these benefits of ideation before applying the concept to cruciformational worshipology in a general sense, and to the elements of liturgy (prayer, preaching, sacrament, and song) in a more specific application.

Regarding the ability to view our world differently by inhabiting the world of the ideated text, Iser notes that entrance into a literary work involves the "construction of a world" to which the text points by providing the syntactical map of structures and signifiers. This gives us a unique standpoint "that would have never come into focus as long as [our] own habitual dispositions were determining [our] orientation."[10] This allows readers, upon lifting their eyes from the world of the text, to gain a fresh perspective on the world outside the text and their own participation in it. In this way art, fiction, literature, and music contain the power not only to represent our world back to us by copying it and projecting it to us through words, sight, and sound but to assist us in re-visioning the world, revising the world, and revolutionizing our experience of it and activities in it. In this way the act of ideating meaning in a text invites us to be immersed in a reality other than our own so that we can escape from the subjective slavery of our preconceived ideas about the world. Through this escape, we become freed from our limited perspectives and subjective perception. Upon our completion of the act of reading, not only can we compare our world with the world of the text, but we can also subvert and change our world with the inspiration achieved through the ideation of a new way of being in the world and seeing the world afforded by the text. "Suddenly," writes Iser, "we find ourselves detached from our world . . . and able to perceive it as an object."[11]

As we begin to apply the concept of the ideation of Jesus Christ through Holy Scripture to what happens in the active life of the worshiping community, we will begin to understand more fully how the Word of God written presents us with the story and structures with which to encounter the Word of God incarnate, Jesus Christ, through the liturgical life of his body, the church.[12]

APPLYING ISER'S THEORY TO THEOLOGY: ENCOUNTERING JESUS IN WORSHIP THROUGH IDEATION

Of prime significance, however, is the ability to make present through ideation that which—or in the case of Jesus, he whom—is not accessible apart from the act of ideation. If what Iser suggests happens in the reading of literature, the reader (while engaged with the text) ideates, assembles, and constructs the meaning of the textual signs and symbols and thereby produces an image otherwise not tangibly present, this has massive implications for Christian worship. In worship, the word about Christ and the knowledge it affords (Col 3:16) leads us to an encounter with Christ himself through liturgical reciprocity of gospel love from the other and to the other.[13] Most people will at the very least grant that the power of music, visual art, literature, and film is so strong that it can, through the profound experience it provides, inspire people to change career paths, end or begin relationships, heal or cause joy or depression, or even ignite a religious conversion. Furthermore, most of us would attribute this powerful ability of art to fictional stories and nonreligious art. How much more, then, should we consider the mighty potential of art to evoke transformation when it provides us with the textual map we can follow to enter into the presence of the living God?

There are numerous models for explaining just how believers experience God and growth in holiness. I do not see ideation as a replacement for other useful models that explain the phenomenon of transformation in Christ. Rather, it is a hermeneutical and philosophical supplement to these theological theories. Ideation proposes to describe one way in which the Word of God made present in worship by the power of the Holy Spirit assists in renewing our minds in the image of God through the embodied, communal encounter with Christ.

As Iser notes, "in reading we think the thoughts of another person" and we become "entangled" with that person through the act and "we actually participate in the text, and . . . are caught up in the very thing we are producing."[14] Thus, through the act of ideating the textual cues provided by the author, we are actually in the presence of the one we ideate and the author is made present in us.[15] The ecclesio-pneumatic ideation of Jesus Christ functions as the means and mechanism by which the knowledge of who God is in Christ is communally made present to us, so that we might enact and receive the cruciform love of God and thereby experience a cruciformation into the image of the cruciform God, Jesus Christ.

The ecclesio-pneumatic ideation of Jesus Christ is the communal encounter of God in Christ that occurs when the Spirit works through the church at worship to make Christ present. This is exclusively through the Spirit-inspired structures and stories about Jesus in the text of the Bible. Though Jesus himself of course exists as God incarnate outside of the texts of Holy Scripture, without the divinely inspired and providentially preserved texts of the Bible, we have no access to him. That is to say, without the Word of God, we have no authoritative, reliable, inspired access to the character, teachings, and person of Jesus Christ, the Word of God. In this sense, as Karl Barth so rightly emphasizes, the Word of God, the Bible, makes present and becomes to us the revelation of the Word of God, Jesus Christ, through the ministries of the scriptural Word in the body of Christ, the church.[16] This is partly why those traditions that work from a low view of Scripture experience such a vacuous and impotent experience of God.

By distorting the biblical witness to Jesus—the only record we have of his life, teaching, death, and resurrection—we substitute the spiritually inspired structures, stories, and apostolic interpretations about him with whatever ideological costume we want him to wear.[17] Thus the "Jesus" ideated in liberal Christianity becomes a gestalt hodgepodge pseudo-Christ who is essentially a cipher for twenty-first-century American politics and boring, stale, suburban, mainline Protestant religious pluralism. Conversely, the Jesus ideated by extreme right-wing readers presents an equally deformed and even dangerous version of Jesus. These extreme right-wing readers arrive at this Frankenchrist not as a result of holding a low view of Scripture or removing verses from it but by inserting ideas alongside the text of the Bible that insidiously attribute non-biblical elements to the person of Jesus[18] In neither case is Jesus ideated; strangely and disturbingly, a false, pseudo, anti-Christ is ideated, which deforms rather than transforms the one who is worshiping him.

In contrast to the liberal guru-hippie-yoga Christ and the right-wing macho-man-Rambo-vengeance Christ, the actual structures, stories, and teachings of Jesus derived from the Word of God must inform the Christ to whom the church submits itself.[19] If we ideate the Jesus of Holy Scripture we will ideate, experience, and encounter not a cartoonish distortion of Jesus but the true, living, transformative Jesus on earth as he is in heaven. The ecclesio-pneumatic ideation of Jesus Christ in and through the worshiping community leads us to the will of God so that we can walk in accord with that will and be transformed into the image of God through knowing God as he really is. And he is made present to us through enacting and receiving—in and as the church—the love that he himself reveals to us in and as Christ. Through ideating the cruciform God of the Bible, we inhabit the cruciform God and he inhabits us.[20] We think his thoughts (as communicated by him, to us, through the Word) not so that we might categorize their content into a collection of facts about him in the form of a systematic theology textbook, but rather so that we might see the world, ourselves, and others afresh from the perspective of the communally embodied person of Jesus. Through embodying the love of Christ in his loving community we experience a cruciformation. By means of the revelatory knowledge that happens when we ideate Jesus Christ in his body, the church, we walk in accord with his ideated image and thereby weave both neural networks in our brain and spiritual networks in our soul. These re-pattern our character in accord with the Spirit-inspired script of the new humanity in Christ to which Holy Scripture witnesses.

Conclusion: Cruciformation Through Liturgical Ideation

As has been stressed throughout this book, the entire process of renewal through the ideation, enactment, and reception of cruciform love is necessarily communal because the love of God itself—that by which and in which and for which we are being renewed—is defined by the others-centered, self-giving, cruciform love of God displayed in the cross and resurrection of Jesus Christ. Cruciformation takes place through the formation of Christlike character in a community. We can observe the communal nature of God's love, on the one hand, in the communal, reciprocal character of the perfect love of the Father, the Son, and the Holy Spirit toward one another as an immanent Trinity in eternity. On the other hand, we observe it in history most profoundly by the love directed toward that which is other than self: namely, the love of God for human beings. Thus, for the church at worship, the word about Christ reveals God himself to us, so that through love we might become like the God who is love—by the other, for the other, and to the glory of God through the other.

The other is, in the most basic sense, the one who is other than ourselves. The gospel of Jesus Christ and the process of cruciformation itself reveals a profound truth: those who are in Christ no longer belong to themselves but exist as new creations only in, through, with, and for the other. Baptism into Christ results in the death of the ego so that the self can become properly re-sensitized for new life in the new creation as a new human being whose entire existence and future subsists in the life and love of Christ. This is necessarily experienced in relation to the other, including both God and other human beings. In the remaining segments of this section I will briefly parse out how a cruciformational theology of worship and the ecclesio-pneumatic ideation of Jesus Christ transforms the church through the liturgical actions of prayer, preaching, sacrament, and song. Then, in the concluding section of the book, I will endeavor to reflect upon how the re-sensitizing ideation of Jesus is meant to bless not only the church but the entire world.

14

THE CRUCIFORMATIONAL PRAYERS OF THE PEOPLE

Ideation Through Supplication

ENCOUNTERING JESUS THROUGH
PREWRITTEN AND SPONTANEOUS PRAYER

There are a number of biblically faithful ways to approach prayer within the liturgical, communal worship of the people of God. Some of our traditions consider spontaneous, Spirit-led prayer to be the only powerful form of prayerful petition and supplication. Other streams of the church make use of the prewritten prayers of the saints through the ages, some of which find their roots in the early church. Most of our congregations likely employ both the evangelical and pietistic practice of Spirit-led prayer and the communal prayer of scripted and Scripture-based prayers such as the Psalms, the prayers of the apostles in the New Testament, and the Lord's Prayer. I will not offer any suggestions or arguments here attempting to vindicate or elevate any one style of praying beyond saying that it is my experience that the combination of pietistic spontaneous petition and the best of the church's prewritten prayer traditions make for a rich worship experience that is rooted in the worship of the church at prayer through the ages while remaining open to the movement of the Holy Spirit in new ways using new words. To this end I recommend the *Book of Common Prayer* (hereafter *BCP*) as a useful worship resource.

The *BCP* contains most of the prayers of the Great Tradition, which is the liturgical catalogue of prayers and liturgies that have their roots in the early church. For Protestants, the *BCP* also contains many beautiful prayers composed by the English Reformer Thomas Cranmer around the time of the Reformation. These prayers (referred to by Anglicans as "Collects" because they are meant to collect our thoughts in the form of a communal prayer) are tied to the various seasons of the church year (i.e., Advent, Christmas, Easter, Lent, etc.) and in most cases are paraphrases or parallels of biblical texts and themes set to prayer. Thus it has been said that the *BCP* is essentially a book that can be described as "the Bible arranged for worship."[1]

Some, however, balk at the idea of using any kind of prewritten material, even if it is used as a bouncing-off point for more improvisational and Spirit-led, spontaneous charismatic prayer. The worry is that using any liturgical prayer or worship material formulated by others before the worship event will result in inauthentic, rote, dead religious activity rather than vibrant, Spirit-filled prayer. Yet while it is certainly the case that some lazy liturgists and nominal Christians can use their liturgical traditions and prayers as a means of engaging in mindless, droning, pedantic, and spiritually lifeless worship, the deficiency in the vibrancy of their worship is not so much due to the fact that they use prewritten resources but rather is rooted in the fact that they engage in worship with these prayers in a cavalier and complacent manner, which eliminates and evacuates the power and passion that comes from the presence of the Holy Spirit. Thus the rejection of prewritten prayers is, I think, unwarranted, unsustainable, and unwise. After all, if spontaneity is the necessary prerequisite for experiencing the powerful ministry of the Holy Spirit, it would follow that such extemporaneity should be applied to all of the segments of worship. Why, if a casual, impromptu approach is most conducive to the movement of the Spirit, should its prioritization and praxis in worship be limited to Spirit-led prayer? If we follow the logic of such a claim all the way to its conclusion, the church ought to be arranging its PowerPoint on the spot during the service "as the Spirit moves." Likewise, even song selection and the rehearsal of songs would be most "authentic" if they were not rehearsed or arranged. It would be better—according to this position—to just show up and let the Spirit move. Selecting songs or working on arrangements would limit the ability of the Spirit to "show up" and be "invited in."[2] In the same way, preaching and sermon preparation would just have to go. How on earth would the Spirit have the space to move "in the moment" if the preacher has already developed an outline or sermon notes ahead of time? Wouldn't these preparatory steps hinder the Spirit's ability to be fully present and fully free?

While a small minority of extremists might argue for the reductio ad absurdum parsed out above, most would see it as hyperbolic, excessive, and undesirable and would likely interpret it as a hindrance rather than a help to the ministry of the Holy Spirit in the worship of the church. Deep down, we all know that some order is necessary in worship, and that through this structure, we create space for the people of God to experience the power of the Holy Spirit. An analogy with music will be helpful here in illustrating this point. Improvisation, the spontaneous creation of new melodies and harmonies, takes place precisely through form and structure rather than apart from it. The form of a twelve-bar blues invites improvisation within a style that helps the improvisor to be free without being totally musically aimless and atonal. Likewise, a chord progression in a major key, or in the Dorian mode, or a tune set to a funk rhythm all invite unique opportunities for improvisational participation while at the same time establishing the ability to play freely within the various structural constraints. Without these structures and starting points one is actually less able to be spontaneous and free. So it is with worship. Some planning in sermon preparation or arranging and re-hearsing worship songs is beneficial because through that preparation, planners set the space, potential, and patterns that actually empower the church to have the most freedom, the most effective spontaneity, and the most powerful spiritually transformative improvisation.

My Will or Thy Will? Whose Will Is Driving and Informing Our Prayer?

Regardless of one's proclivity for or against the inclusion of both spon-taneous and traditional scripted prayer in worship, there is a larger, more important question underneath: Is the content of our prayers being informed by the will of God as revealed through the Word of God? Or are our prayers primarily being formed by our own wills and desires, which are then Christianized by restating our own desires through the cipher and costume of biblical language and themes? Although the clear intention of most Christian worshipers is to pray according to the will of God rather than according to our own will, it remains the case that all of us are likely guilty of—at one time or another—adding the caveat "thy will be done" to our prayers only after we have already stated our own.

If we are seeking to experience the ideation of Jesus Christ through communal prayers, our prayers must issue forth from the will of God as revealed in the Word of God and not—in the first place—from our own hearts, lest we embody, enact, and receive the will and ways of a pseudo-Christ who is really just our own sinful self. The ideation of the sinful self in the place of, under the disguise of, and under the illusory auspices of "Jesus" will never lead to communal or individual transformation in the way of the cross. Prayer that is rooted in the ideation of sin will beget sin. And sin can never transform, it can only ever deform.

This is why the wise and road-worn prayers of the saints through the ages (whether compiled and collected in the *BCP* or elsewhere) provide an ideational safeguard and a scripturally informed starting point for our additional spontaneous prayers. Jesus' paradigmatic instruction on prayer in Matthew 6 makes it clear that the will of God ought to govern and guide our prayers so that God's purposes and kingdom will be made present "on earth as it is in heaven." If we are seeking to pray "in God's will" (which we clearly should be), then even if we do not make use of any of the spiritual resources of the church through the ages, we ought to root our own petitions and supplications firmly in the ways and witness that we find in the Word of God. While discerning God's will certainly includes more than simply referencing Holy Scripture like an encyclopedia, it never requires less than Holy Scripture. Though some conceive of the search for the will of God in life situations as a form of almost Christianized, astrological, magical, mystical, pseudo-Eastern meditation, the truth is that God's will, like all other revelatory communication from God, is mediated exclusively through the Spirit working through his

Word. Thus if we opt out of using any framing prayer from the church in worship, we must be sure to be exceedingly diligent in the task of soaking in the Word with a great degree of regularity and depth. The ideation and embodiment of Jesus requires an access to the mind of Christ (1 Cor 2:16; cf. Phil 1:27; 2:2, 5), which, as we have discovered, is derived from the structures and stories of the Scriptures as they are engaged communally through the transformative power of the Holy Spirit.[3]

CONCLUSION: A PARADIGM FOR CRUCIFORMATIONAL PRAYER IN PHILEMON

We see the pattern of cruciform prayer in Philemon 1–6, in which Paul gives thanks to God for the faith of Philemon, for the church that meets in the house of Archippus, and for their love toward the Lord Jesus and toward one another. Lest this appear as an incidental greeting of Paul that can be quickly passed over, the content of verses 5 and 6 reveals once again the cruciformational pattern of transformation, this time tying the concept directly to the practice of prayer.

Paul writes, "I pray that the sharing of your faith may become effective for the full knowledge of every good thing that is in us for the sake of Christ" (Philem 6). Given a closer look at the Greek (as well as the grammar of the verse and the ubiquitous Pauline and apostolic pattern of cruciformation in the key texts on transformation in the New Testament), we can more accurately translate the verse, "[And I pray] in order that the communion that comes from your faith might become energized by means of knowledge that comes from every good thing done by us thereby resulting in Christ" (my translation). While this translation may at first seem overly cumbersome, it more accurately interprets the Greek text in a theologically compelling way. My rendering of the Greek phrase *hē koinōnia tēs pisteōs* as "the communion which comes from your faith" better explains the function of "faith" to "communion." The prayer then functions to strengthen the unity and communion resulting from the church's joint faith by the experience of an "energy" that occurs through knowledge. This takes the Greek prepositional phrase *en epignōsei* to indicate the instrument or means of achieving the energy, namely knowledge.

It is reasonable to conclude that this knowledge that provides energy is the ideated knowledge of Jesus Christ. This interpretation is made even more sure when in the very next Greek phrase we encounter what is called the "genitive of means," indicating that the good things done by the church result in knowledge that produces the energy that produces the communion experienced in the church. Finally, the prepositional phrase translated by the ESV "for the sake of Christ" (Gk. *eis Christon*) means, in its most basic sense, "unto Christ." Though it can be taken in a number of ways, I have rendered it "resulting in Christ" to more fully express the telic force of the preposition. The point of Philemon 1-6, then, is that our communion in the faith is energized by a knowledge of God. This knowledge is derived from the energy produced in the Spirit-inspired and Spirit-empowered good works that communally manifest the person of Christ. As a result, Christ is formed in us through our communion with one another. Thus, strangely, in this one seemingly insignificant verse in Philemon, we once again discover Paul's cruciformational theology: by walking in the way of God and living a life of active worship in and with the people of God, we are renewed in the image of who God is in Christ. This embodied love—and in this case, love embodied in prayer— through the community of God's love, conforms us to the image of the cruciform God who is love. Pursuing Christlike and Christ-informed prayer in community leads to cruciformation, thus helping to develop the family disposition of love.

15

THE CRUCIFORMATIONAL PREACHING AND SINGING OF THE WORD

Ideation Through Proclamation and Melodic-Harmonic Incarnation

The Word of God preached, read, and sung in the context of the worship of the church is a powerful means of the ideation of Jesus Christ for the cruciformation of the church. The great Orthodox theologian Alexander Schmemann goes so far as to refer to the proclamation of God's Word as a "sacramental act par excellence" precisely because of its power to transform the church and the world.[1] I have chosen to treat both the preaching of the Word and the singing of the Word at the same time because the Bible treats them as coequal mediators of the structures and stories of Holy Scripture. These enable us to encounter the living God through the ideation of Jesus Christ. I will not, however, spend any time comparing preaching styles and/or styles of worship. Instead, I will offer one critique against preaching styles and styles of musical worship that focus on communicating propositions about God as the end goal of worship. This warning must be issued lest we, in our pursuit of biblically faithful, transformative worship, end up worshiping our theological ideas about Jesus rather than allowing them to lead us to the ideation of and transformational encounter with Jesus himself. After having issued this critique, I will then offer a possible way forward in both preaching and singing, which should help us to preach and sing in ways that are biblically faithful but more, lead us to the ideation of Jesus rather than to ideologies constructed in his name.

THE IDEATED PRESENCE OF CHRIST
THROUGH THE PREACHING OF THE WORD

Preaching that views itself primarily as a medium and channel through which to convey data about God must be avoided. Generally speaking, I want to affirm as appropriate and preferable the approach to sermon preparation and delivery usually referred to as expository preaching. In expository preaching, the preacher works verse by verse through passages, and typically through entire books of the Bible over a period of months or even years, seeking to read each text within its context in the particular book of the Bible in which it appears and within the context of its cohesion within the totality of God's revealed, canonical Word. Grammatical-historical exegesis issues forth from a diligent, grammatical-historical study of the original Greek and Hebrew texts. Through this process, the skilled exegete seeks to become cognizant of the force and function of every single word in the text. The task of the grammatical-historical exegete is ultimately to determine the original authorial intention of the passage for the purpose of communicating this to the congregation. In the best-case scenario, original exegesis conducted in preparation for a sermon is then compared with a variety of commentaries spanning Christian theological traditions and epochs to develop the most informed understanding of the various interpretations of a text in the church through the ages. Given that the preacher intends to communicate the Word of God to the congregation, I consider all of the above the benchmark for stepping into the pulpit. This is not to discourage those who might have less access to research materials or to the original languages. However, I want to maintain that if you fall below what I just articulated in terms of your preparation for sermons, in the name of Jesus fill that gap, for the sake of the gospel and the good of your congregation. Just as no one would tolerate a surgeon who was in the habit of conducting unauthorized open-heart surgeries in hotel rooms for practice before he was fully trained in the medical complexities of his craft, so too the church ought not accept preachers who are not seeking to gain the highest degree of mastery in the art of exegesis for the task of rightly dividing the Word of God (2 Tim 2:15).

In the theology of cruciformation, the biblical pattern is that the communal walking in accordance with the will of God leads to a knowledge of God in Christ. The church is renewed through the Jesus who is ideated by that knowledge into the image of God. The ultimate aim of this is to undergo a cruciformation by embodying Christ's love in his loving community. The people of God are thereby perfected through enacting and receiving the love of God in the church. Thus expository preaching, with its emphasis on making present the structures and stories of the Word about Christ, contributes a great deal to the Spirit-inspired ideational structures that lead to the revelation of Jesus Christ himself in the midst of the congregation at worship through the Word.

Yet while I want to affirm the virtue and benchmark of expository preaching, I also want to issue a caution related to expository preaching. The trend in some evangelical circles toward preaching forty-five-minute, exegetical Bible studies from the pulpit and then calling these lectures "sermons" is detrimental to cruciformational worship and the sanctification of the church. Information does not save us; Jesus does. Correct, didactic information transferred from the pulpit to the cerebellum of the congregants certainly can make the church more knowledgeable about Jesus, but exegesis is incomplete if it is not enlivened, illuminated, and empowered by the discernment and exhortation that comes from the Holy Spirit. Exegesis, doctrinal statements, creeds, and confessions are crucial to the church insofar as they are recognized for what they really are—namely, the penultimate map of structures and stories that lead us to Jesus. One's theology about Jesus is only valuable if, by the power of the Holy Spirit in the act of communal worship, it brings about the revelation of Jesus himself.

When we confuse ideas about God for revelation, we act as though our theological systems and statements of faith are ends in themselves rather than means to the end which is participation in God. Theology, when perceived rightly, is not itself revelation, such that we can extract revelation from the Bible, put revelation in a list, compile revelation in a systematic theology textbook, put revelation away when our eyes get sleepy, and even sell used copies of revelation in used bookstores. Rather, the structures, stories, and words of the Bible are meant to witness to the Word, the revelation and ultimate divine self-disclosure of who God is in himself, the crucified and resurrected Christ as he meets us in the act of engaging the words of Scripture about him.

Thus the big idea of any sermon we preach should not ultimately be some random precept, proposition, or life lesson that we can jot down and carry around in our wallet or stick on our fridge like a divinely revealed Post-it note. This would reduce the concept of revelation to the reception of cognitive data. When this happens these big ideas do not function properly as structures and signs through which we can engage in the communal, cruciformational ideation of Jesus Christ. When ideas and divine factoids become the end goal of a sermon rather than the means to the end of encountering Jesus, we do not end up with the ideation of Christ's presence but with the ideology of domineering systems of theology that muzzle the Spirit as he attempts to speak through the Word.

This process is most devastating to the power of the preached Word when it naively and wrongly assumes in advance the infallible nature of a theological system. Ironically, the preacher engaged in such exegesis is actually enslaved by an overly rigid, fundamentalist, immovable, and indubitable theological system, an interpretive grid that blockades off any access to an encounter with Christ in his Word.[2] This error can be widely observed in the preaching, teaching, and conversations of individuals who come at biblical texts having already decided what they can and cannot mean on the basis of their immovable fidelity to a theological system. It is essential that all of the core doctrines of Christianity—about which all orthodox believers agree—be held as firm and immovable Spirit-inspired structures for the ideation of the biblical Jesus. However, when we extend this commitment to entire theological systems (like Calvinism, Arminianism, Roman Catholicism, etc.) with no recourse for any revision or doctrinal reformation on the basis of the Word of God, we cease to be reformed in any sense and are rather enslaved by the systems that we exalt over Scripture.[3] When we then seek to communicate systematic-theological ideas as the ultimate end and aim of our sermons, and when we do so in the name of Jesus to congregations, we extend to them ideas extracted from the Bible and thus make the Bible an irrelevant, obsolete book that becomes increasingly useless as it is surpassed by compiled collections of theological facts extracted from it.

It is this malady that we must be diligent to avoid. Our firm commitment to a high view of the Bible and to expositional preaching must be combined with the conviction that correct ideas about God do not transform unless they become the means to the end of the ideation of Jesus Christ, rather than ends in themselves. Evangelicals in particular tend to be excellent at either leaning heavily into the Spirit so that the Word preached is open to the movement and illumination of the Spirit for their time, place, and cultural contexts or, conversely, turning the sacramental act of preaching into a purely didactic transfer of exegetical lecture notes devoid of the Spirit's power to make these biblical structures, stories, and doctrines about God capable of revealing God himself. It is rare indeed to witness in the same congregation and by the same preacher the ability to rightly handle the Word of God as a serious exegete and the ability to lean into a dependency upon the Holy Spirit through prayer, discernment, meditation, and fellowship, so that the words and ideas about God might point beyond themselves to become a revelation of God in our midst. This, however, is precisely what we must pursue from our pulpit ministries to provide the biblically rooted, Spirit-inspired structures, stories, and spiritual power for experiencing and encountering God through the communal, cruciformational ideation of Jesus Christ.

THE IDEATED PRESENCE OF CHRIST
THROUGH THE SINGING OF THE WORD

When it comes to the singing of the Word, these same warnings persist. It is becoming increasingly more frequent in certain circles of evangelicalism to view music in a merely functional and pedagogical sense rather than in a primarily aesthetic and transformational sense. This need not be approached in an either/or manner. Worship leaders as melodic and harmonic ministers of the Word of God unto the cruciformational ideation of Jesus Christ in the church ought to employ lyrical and musical content that is both biblically faithful and aesthetically compelling. Both of these factors are equally important in the musical worship of God.

The Reformation presents us with several stunning examples of the use of music for praise in pedagogy. Luther himself, having written some forty hymns, was intent on linking his teaching and music together as an integrated whole in order to convey the gospel essentials through a variety of coexisting and cooperating channels. This assisted Luther's congregations in encountering the orthodox, biblical Christ in worship through engaging the ideational structures of orthodox Lutheran theology set to song. Christopher Boyd Brown explains, "Luther had taken care to compose a complete cycle of hymns for all the parts of his Catechism."[4] Furthermore, Brown points out that in the Lutheran town of Joachimsthal, music was used in the schools and proved to teach doctrine in a way that would "stay with them throughout life more effectively than perhaps any other means of instruction."[5] In the Anglican and later Methodist side of the English Reformation we find another worship luminary, Charles Wesley, the brother of John Wesley (the founder of Methodism). Amazingly, Charles Wesley wrote "between six thousand and nine thousand hymns and sacred poems" during his lifetime.[6] Wesley, though often criticized for employing overly subjective language, addressed God through his hymns in a personal, experiential way that follows the pattern of the divinely inspired Psalms. Thus the individualizing tendencies of contemporary worship are not merely capitulation to our twenty-first-century obsession with the self.

It is a frequent concern among many in the church that we avoid the first person pronoun in worship in favor of a more communal "we." Indeed, I have been arguing in this book that the individual in Christ is never separate from the communal body. Yet I think we need to recognize that incorporation into the body does not mean a forfeiture of our individuality into the droning sameness of the collective singular personality in which everything that makes us unique is squashed into a homogeneous "Christian" personality. We are not meant to be robots who through baptism become detached from our former personalities and affections so that we might sing objective, theologically sound treatises to God as if having correct ideas about God were some sort of virtue or end in itself. It is extremely common for the sung component of worship, however, to be viewed by the pastoral staff as a supplementary segment of subliminal indoctrination that piggybacks on the cognitive data conveyed by the lecturer in the pulpit. When this happens, a flesh-eating infection deteriorates the body of Christ by replacing an encounter with Jesus through his body the church with melodically communicated, predetermined theologies about Jesus.

Still, many persist in chastising contemporary Christian worship music for speaking in the first person. In these churches, the leaders consider it a virtue to strip worship of the "I" in favor of the pious "we." Such a move, however, is heretical. In the Psalms, the English pronouns *I, me,* and *my* occur 2,413 times while the corresponding plural pronouns (*we, us,* and *our*) occur a mere 389 times. Likewise, the Hebrew first-person singular verbal form appears 777 times in the Psalms whereas the first-person plural verbal form occurs only 92 times. Contrary to the "plain meaning of Scripture" (tongue fully in cheek) Justin Taylor quotes with approval Jeremy Pierce's article against the use of first-person singular pronouns in modern worship. Pierce (and Taylor) believe that the use of the first person singular in worship "fosters a spirit of individualism, and . . . generates an atmosphere of religious euphoria rather than actual worship of God." Pierce concludes by stating, "Worship should be about God, not about us."[7]

This line of thinking highlights the problem with an intellectualist and cognitivist understanding of worship. Worship conducted in the manner suggested by Pierce and Taylor turns out to be the musical equivalent of a lecture. If anyone wants to argue that we ought to eliminate the individual, experiential encounter with God in communal worship in favor of singing catechetical objective statements of faith about God, they prove themselves to be operating from a biblically deficient theology and a worship praxis that hinders the ideation of Jesus in worship and quenches the collective and individual process of the cruciformation of the church. This approach to worship proves itself to be an aesthetically anemic, transformationally stunted, theologically indefensible slavery to and worship of Enlightenment foundationalism and logical positivism applied to theology. In place of an intellectualist understanding of the liturgical, cruciformational theology of song in worship, we need look no further than the Psalms. The Psalms should be viewed as the divinely inspired paradigm par excellence.

In the Psalms the individual "I" is wonderfully incorporated into the communal "we" of the people of the one God of Israel. The psalmist issues forth his prayer as a member of the community of Israel. When we pray with the psalmist, we pray as individuals who have been incorporated into the one family of Abraham through Jesus Christ (cf. e.g., Gal 3:8-9, 25-29). Thus while it is wise to be discerning about the content and phrasing of our hymnody, it is unnecessary for us to conclude that the use of "I" in worship is always an indicator of individualism. Rather, the inclusion of the "I" in the "we" of gathered worship and in the content of the songs we sing leads to the ecclesio-pneumatic ideation of Jesus Christ and to his cruciformational embodiment in the church, where we enact and receive cruciform love. It is the incarnating of this love, rather than the theologizing about it, that transforms the church and the world.

Conclusion: Ideation Through Proclamation and Melodic-Harmonic Incarnation

The preaching and singing of the Word of God empowers the church to encounter Jesus Christ through his ideated presence in the midst of the community by the power of the Holy Spirit. This experiential encounter with Christ provides the church with an intimate knowledge of Christ as God. Through walking in accord with this knowledge of who God is in Christ, Christians undergo a cruciformation by embodying Christ's love. Whether Christ is made present through sermon or song, the authentic ideation of the living Christ relies upon the activation of the Spirit-inspired structures and stories about him that come alive when they are engaged and illuminated within the community of Christ's love, the church. Therein Christ is made present by the Spirit and the family of God, the church, is cruciformed into the resemblance of God in Jesus Christ.

16

CRUCIFORMATION THROUGH HOLY COMMUNION

Ideation Through Sacramental Participation

Holy Communion or the Lord's Supper is spiritual food for the communal body of Christ by which we participate in one another and in the life of God. It is a sign, seal, and means of grace through which the cruciformation of the church participates in the remembrance of Christ's death and passion through the ingesting of the elements of bread and wine. As has been the custom in this section thus far, there will be no discourse here on the what and how of Holy Communion. There will be no argument concerning the precise mode of Christ's absence from, or his presence in, with, under, or spiritually through the elements. The sole focus of this section will be to understand one core principle of the Holy Communion's manifold mysteries: communion with God and each other is a form of participation in the life of God through the other, by which we grow in the bond that leads to our perfection in the cruciform love of God. To this end we will consider only three texts from the New Testament: namely, Philippians 1:3-11, Acts 2:42, and 1 Corinthians 10:16-17.

These texts taken together concisely demonstrate that communion with God in the sacrament of the Eucharist (or the ordinance of the Lord's Supper) is necessarily linked to the empowering of communion with one another in the body of Christ. This communion with the cruciform God through the sacrament that remembers his defeat of death on the cross and his restoration of life through the resurrection leads to the ideation of Jesus in the church and the cruciformation of her members for the sake of the transformation of the world. Our characters are formed in the image of Christ through our cruciformational participation in the community of communion. Let us begin by considering the logic of Paul in his prayer in Philippians 1:3-11.

HOLY COMMUNION AS THE IDEATION OF JESUS CHRIST

I give thanks to my God on the basis of my remembrance of you, always in every prayer of mine for all of you making my prayer with joy because of your communion [Gk. *epi tēn koinōnia hymōn*] in the gospel from the first day until now, with the result that I am persuaded of this very thing, that he who began a good work in you [pl.] will complete it at the day of Jesus Christ.

Just as it is right for me to think this about you all, because I hold you all in my heart, and because you are all my co-communicants [*synkoinōnous*] of grace, both in my imprisonment and in the defense and confirmation of the gospel. For God is my witness, how I yearn for you all with the deep gut-wrenching affection of Christ Jesus.

And this I pray: that your [pl.] love [sg.] might abound more and more, by means of knowledge and discernment, in order that you might discern what is excellent, in order that you might be pure and blameless on the day of Christ, with the result that you are filled with the fruit of righteousness, that [fruit] which comes through Jesus Christ, to the glory and praise of God. (Phil 1:3-11, my translation)

The first thing to note here is that Paul mentions communion with the Philippians twice in this set of verses. Initially, in Philippians 1:5, this is a "communion, a co-partaking in the gospel." Two verses later, in Philippians 1:7, Paul speaks of his relationship with the Philippians as a co-communion of grace. It is rarely pointed out that the force of the Greek participle *pepoithōs* (lit. "being persuaded") in Philippians 1:6 is to introduce the result of the communion mentioned in the previous verse.

That is to say, it can be grammatically observed here that for Paul, the assuredness that he speaks of when he says that "he who began a good work will complete it at the day of Jesus Christ" is based upon the communion of the gospel (Phil 1:6). Thus it is not an overstatement to say that without the communion of the gospel experienced by the congregants in the church, the certainty that Paul shares about the completion of the work begun would not exist.

Paul is not using the word *koinōnia* ("communion") as a technical term for the Lord's Supper. But as I shall demonstrate momentarily, the concept of communion with one another is inseparably linked in Paul with the reality of communion with God through communal participation in his body and blood through the sacrament of the Eucharist. Before wrapping up with our digest of Philippians 1:1-11, there is one more comment of note concerning the Greek verb translated "completed" in Philippians 1:6. This verb is *epitelesei* which is a compound verb created by the combination of the preposition *epi* with verb *teleō*. *Teleō* is the verbal form of the noun *telos*, which we encountered in Colossians. It can be translated as either "completion" or "perfection." Thus once again we have an example of communal participation in and as the church—this time referred to as *koinōnia* ("communion")—that leads to the perfecting of the work God has begun in the believer. Paul's theology of salvation is cruciformational and requires the Spirit-empowered enactment and reception of cruciform love, love brought about through the ideated presence of Jesus Christ through the communal worship and life of the church.

This connection to a perfection of the church and believers through the embodiment of cruciform love is further demonstrated when Paul shares, in a manner identical to that of Colossians, his prayer that the Philippians' love might abound more and more "by means of knowledge and discernment" (Phil 1:9, my translation). This knowledge leads to the purification and blamelessness that result from the fruit that comes through being part of the righteous people of God (Phil 1:9-11). Now, all of this may appear illuminating and cohesive with the theological trajectory this book has been on since the first chapter. However, one may wonder, what does communion with one another in the church have to do with the sacrament of communion? Should not these two elements of ecclesial life be thought of separately instead of as interrelated theological concepts? Based on Acts 2:42 and 1 Corinthians 10:16-17, such a separation is both impossible and biblically unjustifiable.

Beginning with Acts 2:42, we encounter the classic biblical summary of the earliest church's worship and life after Pentecost. The verse states that the early Christians were devoting themselves "to the apostles' teaching and the fellowship, to the breaking of bread and the prayers" (my translation). It is crucial to point out on the front end that the anchor of the early church's life of worship is the apostolic teaching. Today, of course, we have this very deposit of the faith through the apostolic teachings providentially preserved and inspired by the Holy Spirit in the Old and New Testaments. However, what many readers forget is that the apostolic teaching at the time of the Book of Acts was not in the form of a completed canon, and it was probably not even in any written form yet. Rather, the teachings of the apostles were at this point largely circulating through oral tradition. Eventually the letters of the apostles would, by the guidance of the Holy Spirit working through the church, be identified, collected, recognized, and canonized as Holy Scripture. During the time of which Acts speaks, however, it would be wrong to picture the early church engaged in didactic Bible studies, gaining knowledge from the New Testament and collecting it into theological systems by which they could categorize their knowledge about God. This would have been impossible because there was as of yet no collection of books known as the New Testament. Yet just because there was not yet a New Testament, that does not mean there wasn't a New Testament.

Lest one reread that last sentence searching for a typo, I do in fact mean what I wrote. For as Scott Hahn has argued, before the New Testament was a book it was a sacrament.[1] Jesus teaches his disciples at the Last Supper, well before any epistle about him was ever written, that the cup poured is the *new diathēkē* (covenant, testament) in his blood (Lk 22:20). Although it is usually translated as "covenant," the Greek word here is the word from which we get *testament* as well. It can be translated either way. Translating it as *testament*, as Hahn has done helpfully, points to the fact that the orally transmitted teachings of the apostles and a New

Testament meal, the Eucharist, preceded the structures and stories about Jesus in the books of the New Testament. This can be observed in the grammar of Acts 2:42 in a way that connects the concept of communion with God through the eucharistic activity of the early church to their concept of communion with one another—all in way that demonstrates their inseparability.

The only other use of the phrase "the breaking of bread" (Acts 2:42) in this exact form occurs in Luke 24:35. There Jesus in his resurrection body, though previously veiled to the two disciples with which he was walking, is said to be have been made known to them "in the breaking of the bread." The Greek verbal form *klaō* ("to break") is used in several other contexts that prefigure the Eucharist, such as in the feeding of the five thousand in Matthew 14:19.[2] A text parallel to the Lukan account of the Lord's Supper in Matthew's Gospel reads, "Now as they were eating, Jesus took bread, and after blessing it broke it [Gk. *klaō*] and gave it to the disciples, and said, 'Take, eat; this is my body'" (Mt 26:26; cf. Mk 14:22; Lk 22:19). Thus in the earliest apostolic traditions of the church, the breaking of bread can be shown to be directly related to the celebration of the Lord's Supper.

In 1 Corinthians 10:16-17, Paul brings together the themes of *koinōnia* ("communion") and the breaking of bread in the Lord's Supper. He writes, "The cup of blessing that we bless, is it not a communion [*koinōnia*] in the blood of Christ? The bread that we break [*klaō*], is it not a communion [*koinōnia*] in the body of Christ?" (my translation). Thus Paul roots the concept of communion with God and with one another in the New Testament eucharistic meal which preceded the New Testament book. Coming around full circle to Acts 2:42, it is then not surprising to discover that in that passage the word *koinōnia* (communion) is in grammatical apposition to the phrase "the breaking of bread." What this means is that the words appear directly next to each other in the same gender, number, and case (feminine, singular, dative) in the original Greek, thus indicating that they are referring to the same phenomenon. The grammar indicates that there is, so to speak, an equal sign between the two phrases. Thus in Acts 2:42 the communion/participation is the breaking of bread. The two concepts are inseparable.

In conclusion, this theological investigation into the sacrament of Holy Communion as a vehicle of liturgical ideation of Jesus Christ unto cruciformation brings with it a challenge to the contemporary worshiping church. If, as it has been shown, the celebration of the Lord's Supper was not merely an occasional tag-on to be dealt with quarterly or monthly as a supplement to the more central and important role of preaching, but was rather a central, significant, and inseparable predecessor to the New Testament text, then it follows that our treatment and practice of the sacrament in the context of the worshiping church ought to correspond to this biblical, apostolic faith and practice. Communion should be frequent and central to our worship, and it should follow closely with the structure of the pattern displayed by Christ at the Last Supper. These are the words of Christ, spoken in conjunction with the elements, for the ideation of his presence—all so that the church may grow in the perfection of his love in and as his body. This is how we embody Christ in his loving community and are thereby transformed into the image of his cruciform love. The content of communion is Christ himself, the context is the church, and the result is cruciformation.

Some may object, saying, "Practicing the Lord's Supper frequently will degrade the special, reverential nature of the act by making it too commonplace." To those who make this argument, I offer the following challenge: apply that logic consistently if you use it at all. It would follow, given that logic, that preaching every week could get predictable and could be taken for granted. Or likewise, singing and musical worship, it could be argued, would be much more powerful if done only once per quarter. I could carry on the anti-logic of this position for ages. Refraining from a key apostolic sacrament that is central to the ideational, cruciformational presence of Jesus Christ in the church in the name of pragmatism is as unwise as it is unbiblical.

CONCLUSION—CRUCIFORMATION THROUGH IDEATION: THE ENACTMENT AND RECEPTION OF CRUCIFORM LOVE THROUGH THE IDEATION OF THE CRUCIFORM GOD

The ideational practices of worship exist for the purpose of the cruciformation of the church into the image of the God who is love. Through these liturgical practices we are transformed. This is not simply knowledge about God; it is the communally arrived at, experiential knowledge of God himself. We do not primarily arrive at this knowledge through a collection or assortment of correct theological ideas about God designed to result merely in statements of faith. Rather, we arrive at the knowledge of God through biblically faithful doctrine—not as an end in itself but as a means to the end of the ideation of the presence of Jesus Christ in our midst. It is through the power of the Spirit working through the Word faithfully prayed, preached, sung, and consumed in the sacrament of Holy Communion that the Spirit-inspired structures and stories about Christ lead our minds to encounter him (individually and collectively) through the communal engagement with the Word in the church.

As we have seen, the communal nature of the church does not eliminate or flatten the uniqueness of the individual but rather sets it free to serve the other in their midst in the church. In so doing, the enactment of divine love toward the other and the reception of divine love from the other transforms and renews us in the image of the God who is love. What remains to be seen is how the love of God embodied in the church is meant to transform the entire world. The cruciformation of the church is not meant to be an end itself. It is meant to engage in a communal act of cruciform restoration and reconciliation, a cruciformission. It is toward this final component of the cruciformation of the cosmos through the agency of the body of Christ that we now turn.

PART 6

CRUCIFORM
MISSION

17

CRUCIFORMISSION

Reconciled Reconcilers

The Church constitutes itself through love and on love, and in this world is to "witness" to Love, to re-present it, to make Love present. Love alone creates and transforms: it is therefore, the very "principle" of the sacrament.

ALEXANDER SCHMEMANN

The cruciformation of the church exists to create and empower a people who have been transformed by the embodiment of the gospel so that they might become agents of transformation in the world. Thus the cruciformation of the church into the image of the cruciform God overflows into a cruciformission by which the structures and stories of the biblical witness to the cruciform God are infused into the structures and stories of the world, creating eschatological, transformational tension and collision. Thus the reality of the new creation initiated by God in the resurrection of Jesus Christ is made manifest. The church becomes a contradiction, or as I have argued, a cruciform counterculture comprised of what Shane Claiborne refers to as "holy troublemakers," whose aim and mission is the cruciformation of the status quo of the kingdoms and cultures of this world.[1]

Moltmann captures the heart of the subversive and revolutionary impulse that arises from a heart that is in the process of being transformed
by the self-giving love of Jesus. He writes, "Faith, whenever it develops
into hope, causes not rest but unrest, not patience but impatience. It does
not calm the unquiet heart, but is itself this unquiet heart in man. Those
who hope in Christ can no longer put up with reality as it is, but begin to
suffer under it, to contradict it."[2] Elsewhere Moltmann refers to the disposition and mission of the cruciform church as that which objects to a
complacent acceptance of "the religion of humble acquiescence in the
present." Instead, the church that is walking in the way of the cross must
object to the present world order and be empowered by a "world-trans-
forming" hope that engages and confronts the powers of oppression, sin,
and death in the world.[3]

Only through this "gospel inertia" will the church be living in step and
sequence with the hope it proclaims. We commit ourselves to trust and
act in the present by the power of the Holy Spirit on the basis of the
promises of the living God, in accord with the hope that fully awaits only
in the future.[4] This hope points toward nothing less than the restoration,
reconciliation, and spiritual renovation of all things in Jesus Christ. And
this happens precisely through the agency of the Holy Spirit cruciforma-
tionally working in and through the church for the life, redemption, and
cruciformation of the world. The church is not merely a religious insti-
tution into which we are indoctrinated by spiritual ideologies that put us
into a theologically induced coma in which we are unable to contradict
the world. Rather, the church is meant to be a countercultural, cruciform
ecclesia (assembly) of reconciled reconcilers who creatively reshape the
world, restructure the narratives, and rewrite life in accordance with the
cruciform love of God in Christ.[5]

How, though, does the worship and ecclesio-pneumatic ideation of
Jesus Christ make itself present to a world that is quite often at total odds
with the teachings of Christ? While the principle of enacting and ideating
the love of Christ toward the world is the clear call of Holy Scripture, the
methods by which this cruciformission can be accomplished vary. In fact,
I think it would be a mistake even to attempt to categorize and list the
various methodologies and activities pertaining to cruciformission. In so

doing, we would preempt the power and priorities of the Holy Spirit in his process of revealing and illuminating the unique, indigenous missional opportunities to which he desires to call each of us—within our own local contexts—for the sake of the transformation of the world through the ministry of the gospel. Once again, Shane Claiborne is helpful here:

> Now, while there are a million different ways to respond to this invitation, we do see compelling patterns in the gospel. So even if we don't all respond in the exact same way, we can all, for example, see the suffering of this world as something we are called to enter into instead of flee from. We can reject the patterns of, for example, suburban sprawl that are often built around moving away from pain, or away from neighborhoods of high crime, or away from people who don't look like us, and respond instead to the gospel inertia that invites us to enter into that pain. So this means we also have to challenge some of those patterns of consumerism and insulation, and sprawl, and homogeneity.[6]

Thus the paradigm of redemption by which the cruciformed church is called to bring about the cruciformation of the cosmos is a guiding principle and pattern, rather than a particular application or approach for the renewal of all things. The particular applications of cruciformissional ideation rely on the pneumatic discerning of the Spirit from the heart of the local community and the local church rather than on a pragmatic dictating of successful ministry strategies.

To return to a theme established in the first chapter, we can now say that the presence of the proleptic park of the new creation in our world is entirely dependent upon the cruciformissional ideation of Jesus Christ. To paraphrase Schmemann, the church is constituted by love and is in this world a witness to love. The church is called to participate in the transformation and renewal of all things by re-presenting love, by making love present. The love of Christ is made present through ideation and embodied enactment. Again, without going into specific details, I will at least say that I am increasingly drawn toward the challenge of the local expression, ideation, and enactment of the cruciform love of Jesus to the world. Funding large ministry initiatives is, I think, a definite part of the

CHRIS LLEWELYN OF REND COLLECTIVE

We are all storytellers and we pretty much have no choice in the matter. We are not all authors, writers, or journalists, we may not have children who ask us to spin tall tales to them before they go to sleep, but we are storytellers nonetheless. Our lives are broadcasting a narrative at all times, and this is beyond our control. But we can choose what kind of story.

The type of story that the Scriptures ask us as Christians to tell comes under a simple yet utterly transformational heading: "Good News." The transmission of good news is our mission as believers. It is crazy that the word *evangelism* has become an awkward and uncomfortable term in the world today. It simply means sharing good news—people love good news!

Our lives are a blank page on which to craft an astonishing tale of the good news of God's goodness. It is through living this mission that we see the bad, the mediocre, and the lifeless stories of this world transformed into the image of the "Author and Perfecter."

So where do we begin? Francis of Assisi is thought to have said, "Preach the gospel at all times and when necessary use words."

Let's use everything we do to "preach" good news.

Let's use our art to draw attention to beauty and create moments of holy wonder.

Let's use our workplaces as arenas for the display of God's heart for excellence.

Let's be kind when apathy is tempting and rewrite someone's chapter.

Let's talk about Jesus Christ.

Let's be good storytellers.

---

equation. Much good can be accomplished from sacrificially supporting established agencies in the task of bringing redemption and healing to every corner of this earth in the name of Jesus. However, participation in such endeavors does not seem sufficient in itself to attend to the fullness of the Christian vocation of being reconciled reconcilers. I am increasingly drawn toward a vision of cruciformission in which the task of reconciliation to which Christ calls the church is infused into the matrix of the DNA of our daily lives in particular times and places, in relationships with particular people, problems, and cultures. A vision of cruciformission that exalts the transformative power and possibilities of our vocations, in the midst of our neighborhoods and in the sanctuaries of our homes, allows us to avoid a mentality that views the missionary activity of reconciliation as the work of superheroes.

Reconciliation is the work of ordinary folks who are empowered to enact the love of Christ through an invested life by a cruciform long obedience in the same direction. The embodiment of Christ's love is the content of the cruciformission, the church is the context, and the result is not only the cruciformation of the church but the cruciformation of the whole cosmos. That is, the permanence and investedness of cruciformity in community is a simple and steady—but profoundly catalytic—means toward the reliable and reoccurring, ideated and incarnated presence of Jesus to effect the cruciformation of local cultures, customs, and cities. Moltmann views sin and slavery as "the self-closing of open systems against their own time and potentialities" and salvation as "the divine opening of closed systems."[7] By this statement he points to the limiting nature and power of sin, which negates life's ability to flourish by closing off humanity's access to what life is meant to be. When sin and the self-closing of systems restricts and desensitizes individuals, this results in the endemic and Adamic degradation of the local cultures they inhabit and to which they contribute as world-shapers.

Thus I am challenging and calling you to be reconciled reconcilers. I am calling us all to be those who, through our participatory cruciform permanence in a place with a particular people, engage in reshaping the world. We do this through the ideated presence of Jesus Christ as the Spirit-empowered openers of closed systems, reestablishing the reality of hope in the present. We re-form the world by enabling it to reimagine itself not as it is in its present brokenness but as it will be in its proleptic blessedness.

NOTES

Preface and Acknowledgments

[1]The phrase "beautiful, terrible world" is borrowed from the Decemberists' album *What a Terrible World, What Beautiful World.*

[2]Episcopal Church, *The Book of Common Prayer and Administration of the Sacraments and Other Rites and Ceremonies of the Church: Together with the Psalter or Psalms of David According to the Use of the Episcopal Church* (New York: Church Hymnal Corp, 1979), 94.

1 The Stories that Transform (or Deform) Us and the World

[1]Cf. Roger Olsen, *Reformed and Always Reforming: The Postconservative Approach to Evangelical Theology* (Grand Rapids: Baker Academic, 2007), 114: "Truth cannot be captured and kept in a humanly derived doctrinal expression or system closed to revision and reform." Olsen argues against a view of theology that views that Bible as a source book for the collection and retrieval of theological facts about God. This, he argues, would make the Bible eventually obsolete. See ibid., 43, 54, 72, 81, 82, 88, 102.

[2]Cf. Emil Brunner, *Truth as Encounter* (Philadelphia: Westminster Press, 1943). Brunner gives an in-depth argument about revelation as an encounter with a person rather than a collecting of facts: "Truth as encounter is not truth about something, not even truth about something mental, about ideas. Rather is it truth which breaks in pieces the impersonal concept of truth and mind, truth can be adequately expressed only in the I-Thou form" (ibid., 24). Also, "The self-revelation of God is no object, but wholly the doing and self-giving of a subject—or, better expressed, a Person. A Person who is revealing himself, a Person who demands and offers Lordship and fellowship with himself, is the most radical antithesis to everything that could be called object or objective" (ibid., 109). This is contrary to the view of Charles Hodge as quoted in Nancey Murphy, *Beyond Liberalism & Fundamentalism: How Modern and Postmodern Philosophy Set the Theological Agenda* (Valley Forge: Trinity Press International, 1996), 16. Hodge writes: "The duty of the Christian theologian is to ascertain, collect, and combine all the facts which God revealed in the Bible." This view confuses the collection

of facts *about* a person with the revelation and encounter *of* the Person, Jesus Christ, through those facts. The important and primary focus should be on the one to whom the facts point and the one whom they make present, rather than the facts in and of themselves as standalone propositions.

[3]I hate peanut butter but I love Reese's Pieces candy which technically contains peanut butter. Let those who have ears to hear, hear.

[4]Kudos to the author of the Gospel of Mark.

[5]Walter Wink, *Engaging the Powers: Discernment and Resistance in a World of Domination* (Minneapolis: Fortress Press, 1992), 23.

[6]Ibid., 30.

[7]The phrase "social imaginary" is also commonly used to describe this phenomenon. It is associated with Charles Taylor. Recently, the concept of the social imaginary has been taken up by James K. A. Smith in *Desiring the Kingdom: Worship, Worldview, and Cultural Formation* (Grand Rapids: Baker Academic, 2009) to contribute to the task of informing a constructive theology of Christian education and worship. By "social imaginaries," Smith refers to a mode of experiencing the world that is not primarily based on gathered facts, data, and fully cohesive and comprehensive worldviews that precede action but rather on the imagination, and the stories, practices, and plausibility structures that precede our analytical thought about them and their subsequent categorization into systematic structures of thought, i.e., worldviews. Thus Smith describes the social imaginary as "an affective, noncognitive understanding of the world: which is described as an imaginary (rather than a theory) because it is fueled by the stuff of the imagination rather than the intellect; it is made up of, and embedded in, stories, narratives, myths and icons" (ibid., 66). I agree with and draw upon the work of James K. A. Smith in *Desiring the Kingdom*. There he refers to our patterns of participation in the world as "liturgies" which are "pre-theoretical" ways of experiencing and acting in the world. He states, "Liturgies—whether 'sacred' or 'secular'—shape and constitute our identities by forming our most fundamental desires and our basic attunement to the world. In short, liturgies make us certain kinds of people, and what defines us is what we love" (ibid., 25).

[8]I am using the term *the other* interchangeably and as a synonym for the phrases "someone other than oneself," "each other," or "one another."

2 THE WORLD THAT WE SHAPE AND THE WORLD THAT SHAPES US

[1]Michael Gorman's book *Cruciformity: Paul's Narrative Spirituality of the Cross* (Grand Rapids: Eerdmans 2001) revolutionized my own understanding of Paul, the New Testament, and Jesus on the nature of the Christian life and salvation. There Gorman defines and explicates the concept of cruciformity, arguing that "Christ's death for us both demonstrates and defines divine love. . . . The term

'cruciformity,' from 'cruciform' (cross-shaped) and 'conformity,' may be defined as conformity to Jesus the crucified Messiah" (ibid., 66). Further, cruciformity is "participating in and embodying the cross" (ibid., 67). Also, "Cruciformity is an ongoing pattern of living in Christ and of dying with him that produces a Christlike (cruciform) person. Cruciform existence is what being Christ's servant, indwelling him and being indwelt by him, living with and for and according to him, is all about, for both individuals and communities" (ibid., 48-29). Elsewhere Gorman defines cruciformity as "the rejection of selfish exploitation of status in favor of self-giving action" and as "the rights-renouncing, others-regarding, cruciform humility and love that are needed for existence in the Christian community." Michael Gorman, "The Cross in Paul: Christophany, Theophany, Ecclesiophany" in *Ecclesia and Ethics: Moral Formation and the Church*, ed. E. Allen Jones III, John Frederick, John Anthony Dunne, Eric Lewellen, and Janghoon Park (London: Bloomsbury T&T Clark, 2016), 21-40. See also Michael Thompson, *Clothed with Christ: The Example and Teaching of Jesus in Romans 12.1–15.13*, Journal for the Study of the New Testament Supplement Series 59 (Sheffield: Sheffield Academic Press, 1991), 239; Frank J. Matera, *New Testament Ethics: The Legacies of Jesus and Paul* (Louisville: Westminster John Knox Press, 1996), 107, 160, 170, 174, and 179; and Richard B. Hays, *The Faith of Jesus Christ: The Narrative Substructure of Galatians 3:1–4:11* (Grand Rapids: Eerdmans, 2002), xxix: "'Those who are in Christ are shaped by the pattern of his self-giving death. He is the prototype of redeemed humanity."

[2]The use of the phrase "seduction and distraction" in reference to the culture is something I picked up from Professor John Jefferson Davis in his 2008 Christian Ethics course lectures at Gordon-Conwell Theological Seminary in South Hamilton, MA.

[3]The idea of the gospel "contradicting the world" is derived from Jürgen Moltmann, *Theology of Hope: On the Ground and Implications of a Christian Eschatology* (Minneapolis: Fortress Press, 1993), 1, 3, 4, 5, 8, and 10.

3 AN INTRODUCTION TO CRUCIFORMATION
(OR, TOWARD A THEOLOGY OF "FAMILY RESEMBLANCE")

I am taking up the phrase "family resemblance" from Michael J. Gorman, *Cruciformity: Paul's Narrative Spirituality of the Cross* (Grand Rapids: Eerdman's, 2001), 16. There he explains how Jesus' sacrifice on the cross is an act of family resemblance demonstrating the love of God the Father.

[1]Leonardo Blair, "Victoria Osteen Ripped for Telling Church 'Just Do Good for Your Own Self'; Worship Is Not for God, 'You're Doing it for Yourself,'" *CP Church & Ministries, The Christian Post*, August 30, 2014, www.christianpost.com/news/victoria-osteen-ripped-for-telling-church-just-do-good-for-your-own-self-worship-is-not-for-god-youre-doing-it-for-yourself-125636/.

[2]I understand the heart behind the "audience of one" language. It is not always meant to convey a performance mentality. Rather, the intention is to emphasize the singular nature of the receiver of the worship, namely God. I am not at all critiquing that idea; on the contrary, I support it. My criticism of the phrase is really focused on the language of an *audience*, which, to most people—despite the intention of the person using the phrase—conjures images of a concert and a performance.

[3]Lest anyone missed it or forgot, it is delightful to recall the ridiculousness that ensued in November of 2015 revolving around Starbucks's removal of Christmas images from their seasonal coffee cups. Self-proclaimed evangelist Joshua Feuerstein contributed to the "war on Christmas" when he posted on Facebook that "Starbucks REMOVED CHRISTMAS from their cups because they hate Jesus." The video went viral through social media. Oh, how I love the glorious Internet. See Karen Workman, "Everyone Is Upset, or Not Upset, About Christmas," *New York Times*, November 12, 2015, www.nytimes.com/2015/11/13/nytnow/everyone -is-upset-or-not-upset-about-christmas-ads-already.html.

[4]If you asked Carl, "Who are the Bogus Poets?" He would say: "Well, like, you've probably never heard of them because they are sort of, like, underground and stuff. I guess you could say they sound like Fugazi before they sold out and went corporate. They're sort of like postambient folk-core with a hint of retro-trance. But, then again, that's their earlier stuff. Their newer stuff sounds more like Dylan meets the Talking Heads meets the Cars meets Hüsker Dü."

[5]My own view is that the most critical reading of Colossians indicates that the evidence presented against Pauline authorship of the epistle is not sufficient to deny that the epistle was, in fact, written by Paul. The view that affirms Pauline authorship of the epistle, which was the majority view in antiquity and then became a minority view in the nineteenth and twentieth centuries, is experiencing a resurgence in scholarly support in the twenty-first century, although there is currently no consensus on the authorship of Colossians.

[6]Gorman, *Cruciformity*, 16.

[7]The great philosopher Aristotle recognized this basic phenomenon when he wrote *The Nicomachean Ethics*. In that work Aristotle essentially argues that our characters are formed through our behaviors. Over time the result of the frequent practice of our behavioral responses forms habits within us. Eventually our character, formed in a large part by our actions, becomes a set of habits that exist within us and which act in an almost automatic fashion. For example, a consistent response of impatience from an individual yields, over time, the character trait of impatience. How does one become an impatient person? To a great degree, Aristotelian ethics (otherwise known as "virtue ethics") would say that an impatient person becomes impatient by reacting in

an impatient way frequently over an extended period of time. See Aristotle, *The Nichomachean Ethics*, trans. J. A. K. Thomson (London: Penguin Books, 2004).

[8]I'm picking up this phrase from the title of Eugene Peterson's excellent book on discipleship titled *A Long Obedience in the Same Direction: Discipleship in an Instant Society* (Downers Grove: InterVarsity Press, 2000).

4 Cruciform Knowledge

[1]Side note: I would say that one out of every ten times I brush my teeth I end up mistakenly using Liam's bubblegum toothpaste. One would think it tastes amazing; it doesn't. It is totally gross and makes for a subpar brushing experience.

[2]This is my own translation from the original Greek.

[3]Cf. a similar critique made in N. T. Wright, *Virtue Reborn* (London: SPCK, 2010), 46. In the US the book is titled *After You Believe: Why Christian Character Matters* (New York: HarperOne, 2010).

[4]So too Thomas Aquinas, *Commentary on Colossians*, trans. Fabian Larcher, O.P., http://dhspriory.org/thomas/SSColossians.htm#12, (#21): "And *after* one has borne fruit, an increase in knowledge follows, and increasing in the knowledge of God; *for as a result of eagerly accomplishing the commands of God, a person is disposed for knowledge*" (my emphases).

[5]References to "knowledge of the truth" in a more doctrinal sense do also occur in the New Testament. They are most frequent in the Pastoral Epistles (e.g., 1 Tim 2:4; 2 Tim 2:25; 3:7; Tit 1:1; Heb 10:26). Other similar passages that parallel this usage of knowledge would include biblical references to the importance of holding to sound doctrine. These occur, for example, in Rom 16:17; Eph 4:14; 1 Tim 1:3, 10; 4:6; 6:3; and Tit 1:9; 2:1, 10. Cf. Emil Brunner, *Truth as Encounter* (Philadelphia: Westminster Press, 1943). He notes that doctrine is "dead, powerless, and wholly without worth" if it is viewed as an end in itself rather than the means to the end of encountering God. Rather, doctrine, Brunner argues, is meant to be a tutor that brings us to Christ. He notes that the confusion of doctrine, dogma, and confessional formulas, which tell us things about God with the Word of God himself, Jesus Christ, results in "a tragic blight that lies over the whole history of the Church" (ibid., 139). Also, "Faith is not primarily faith in something true—not even in the truth 'that' Jesus is the Son of God; *but it is primarily trust in and obedience to this Lord and Redeemer himself*, and on the ground of this trust, fellowship with him according to his Word" (ibid., 153 [my emphasis]).

[6]See Lk 10:22 and Jn 10:1-21; 14:7, 9, 17, 20, 31; 15:18; 16:3; 17:3, 23. Cf. 2 Pet 1:3-4, which states that we become "partakers of the divine nature" *through knowledge of God*. Cf. Eph 1:17, in which Paul prays that we might receive "a spirit of wisdom and revelation *by means of knowledge of him*" (Gk. *en epignōsei autou*); cf. Phil 1:9, "it is my prayer that your (pl.) love (sg.) may abound more and more,

by means of knowledge and discernment" (my translation). See also 1 Cor
2:11-16; Phil 3:10; and Heb 8:11.

[7]See R. T. France, *The Gospel of Matthew* (Grand Rapids: Eerdmans, 2007), 293:
"The doubling address draws attention to it as important in its own right." Also,
"to 'know' is commonly used in biblical literature for much more than acquaintance or recognition; it denotes a relationship . . . 'I never knew you' means in
effect that he does not acknowledge them as part of his true family" (ibid., 295).
When my students ask me about this verse I always try to convince them that the
reason Jesus rejects these disciples is simply because they said the magic word
(i.e., Jesus' title as *Lord*) only twice rather than three times. Everyone knows that
you are supposed to say the magic word thrice in order for the wish to be effica-
cious. This principle can be clearly observed in the 1988 motion picture *Beetlejuice* in which, in order to conjure up the bio-exorcist demon guy to help the dead
deal with the living who have taken over their home, the main characters have to
say his name three times: "Beetlejuice! Beetlejuice! Beetlejuice!" If the disciples
had just followed the Beetlejuice formula, Jesus would have been fine with them
and probably invited them to play a game of cards or to go bowling or something.

[8]James K. A. Smith in *Desiring the Kingdom: Worship, Worldview, and Cultural
Formation* (Grand Rapids: Baker Academic, 2009), 32-33. Cf. 216, on which he
quotes from then Roman Catholic Cardinal Joseph Ratzinger who articulates the
same idea: "Christianity is not an intellectual system, a collection of dogmas, or a
moralism. Christianity is instead an encounter, a love story; it is an event." "Homily
for Msgr Luigi Giussani," *Communio: International Catholic Review* 31 (2004): 685.

[9]Cf. George Montague T.S.M, *Growth in Christ: A Study in Saint Paul's Theology
of Progress* (Fribourg: St. Paul's Press, 1961), 199: "One grows in the knowledge
of God by living in communion with his will, so that in Col 1:9f. Paul asks that
his readers first be filled with a knowledge of God's will, *so that through worthy
living out of it, they may grow in the knowledge of God himself.* Paul is in the
tradition of the Old Testament in which knowledge means intimate communion with the person or thing known, a commitment of one's whole being
and not merely an act of the mind" (my emphasis).

[10]The ESV translates the Greek word here as "maturity." However, I do not think
this rendering adequately expresses the transformative, supernatural nature of
the process that is taking place.

5 CRUCIFORM PERFECTION

[1]See Michael Gorman in reference to the use of *en Christō* in Colossians as at
once referring to the sphere, power, and lordship of Christ. He writes, "The
language is not so much mystical as it is spatial: to live within a 'sphere' of
influence. The precise meaning of the phrase varies from context to context,
but to be 'in Christ' principally means to be under the influence of Christ's

power, especially the power to be conformed to him and his cross, *by partici-pation in the life of a community that acknowledges his lordship.*" Michael J. Gorman, *Cruciformity: Paul's Narrative Spirituality of the Cross* (Grand Rapids: Eerdmans, 2001), 36 (my emphasis, see also 37). See also Stanley Hauerwas, *The Peaceable Kingdom: A Primer in Christian Ethics* (London: SCM Press, 1984), 75: "Notice that this life is fundamentally a social life. We are 'in Christ' insofar as we are part of a community pledged to be faithful to this life as the initiator of the kingdom of peace."

[2]The Greek for this is *en Christō* which is typically translated "in Christ." Cf. Jerry L. Sumney, *Colossians: A Commentary* (Louisville: Westminster John Knox Press, 2008), 109: "In Christ designates the sphere in which God perceives believers at judgment. It is also the sphere in which they conduct their lives now." Barth/Blanke seem to take it as trust in Christ, by which we remain or depart, are obedient or disobedient to Christ and that this is the nature of perfection. Markus Barth and Helmut Blanke, *Colossians: A New Translation with Introduction and Commentary*, trans. Astrid B. Beck (New York: Doubleday, 1994), 267-68. This is contra Schweizer who thinks the phrase here is equivalent to the adjective "Christian." Eduard Schweizer *The Letter to the Colossians: A Commentary* (London: SPCK, 1982), 112.

[3]Cf. Eduard Lohse, *Colossians and Philemon* (Philadelphia: Fortress Press, 1971), 10: "The formula 'in Christ' (ἐν Χριστῷ), in Col as in the other Pauline letters, expresses that those who are 'in Christ' are shaped by the Christ-event, or live in the dominion of the exalted Lord" and that the brothers in Christ "are the Christian brothers who, as members of the body of Christ, *are drawn together into a community*" (my emphasis). See also Murray J. Harris, *Colossians & Philemon—Exegetical Guide to the Greek New Testament* (Grand Rapids: Eerdmans, 1991), 73: "Here ἐν Χριστῷ means either . . . in union with Christ . . . or . . . *as a mature member of Christ's body . . . the individual and corporate senses respectively*" (my emphasis).

[4]The Greek word is *energeō*, hence my translation "energized."

[5]Cf. Phil 3:10-12, "that I may know him and the power of his resurrection, and may share his sufferings, becoming like him in his death, that by any means possible I may attain the resurrection from the dead. Not that I have already obtained this or am already perfect, but I press on to make it my own, because Christ Jesus has made me his own." The theme of perfection is also central to the epistle to the Hebrews. This is pertinent to the discussion, though most scholars take Hebrews to be written by someone other than Paul. See, for example, Heb 2:10; 5:9; 6:1; 7:28; 9:9, 11; 10:1, 14; 11:40; and 12:2, 23. See also 1 Pet 1:9 where the *telos* (i.e., outcome, aim, completion, *perfection*) of our faith is overtly labeled as "the salvation of . . . [our] souls."

[6]Gk. *ton neon ton anakainoumenon eis epignōsin kat' eikona tou ktisantos auton.*
[7]NRSV, NASB, ESV, and NIV translate this phrase as the "old self" while the KJV, NKJV, Douay-Rheims, and I render it "the old man." RSV stands out in its translation of the phrase as "the old nature," which seems to lean more toward a theological anthropology than the idea of individual existential existence (so, e.g., NIV) or former representation and corporate way of life (so, e.g., KJV and my translation).
[8]I am in general agreement with Wright, who speaks of the idea as being of one moving into a different sphere and way of life, and of this sphere as New Humanity, or life "patterned on the Messiah who is himself the true Man." N. T. Wright, *The Epistles of Paul to the Colossians and to Philemon: An Introduction and Commentary* (Leicester: Inter-Varsity Press, 1988), 138. See also Moule: "These phrases do not merely mean 'one's old, bad character' and 'the new, Christian character' respectively, as an individual's condition: they carry deeper, wider, and more corporate associations, inasmuch as they are part of the presentation of the Gospel in terms of the two 'Adams,' the two creations. . . . Thus the terms 'the old humanity,' 'the new humanity' derive their force not simply from some individual change of character, but from a corporate recreation of humanity; and what enables the individual to become transformed from selfishness to a growing effectiveness as a useful member of a group is precisely his 'death' in regard to one type of humanity—the great, collectively unredeemed Man—and his 'resurrection' into another: we are back, once more, at the language of baptismal initiation and incorporation." C. F. D. Moule, *The Epistles of Paul the Apostle to the Colossians and to Philemon* (Cambridge: Cambridge University Press, 1958), 119-20. Also, per Barth/Blanke, the old self is "Adam as representative of the old order, the sin of degenerate humanity, and the new self is Christ as representative of the new, redeemed order of humanity." Barth/Blanke, *Colossians*, 410-12.
[9]Thompson exegetes these dual themes of love and community in Romans: "The law of Christ is fulfilled by bearing one another's burdens, a concrete act of love for the neighbor," and "love is worked out in the life of the church." Michael Thompson, *Clothed with Christ: The Example and Teaching of Jesus in Romans 12.1-15.13*, Journal for the Study of the New Testament Supplement Series 59 (Sheffield: Sheffield Academic Press, 1991), 131. Cf. Frank J. Matera, *New Testament Ethics: The Legacies of Jesus and Paul* (Louisville: Westminster John Knox Press, 1996), 133-34, 198. Helpful as well is Robinson's account of Hebrew corporate representation in H. Wheeler Robinson, *Corporate Personality in Ancient Israel* (Edinburgh: T&T Clark, 1981). He shows that it was not that the Hebrews were unaware of individuality, but that they were "more conscious of being one of the group" (ibid., 45). See also, on the corporate nature of the old covenant, ibid., 51: "Observe that the covenant is with the

nation, not with the individual Israelites except as members or representatives of the nation." On the use of the body metaphor for the church by Paul, Robinson writes: "This is the most explicit utterance of the Bible concerning the relation of the group and the individual. It implies a new kind of individual, but one who, like the true Israelite of old, could never be divorced from his social relationship" (ibid., 58). See also Meeks on the primary aim of NT ethical documents as addressed "not to individuals but to communities." Wayne Meeks, *The Origins of Christian Morality—The First Two Centuries* (London: Yale University Press, 1993), 5.

[10]The only other use of the verb *rhizoō* "to be rooted" by Paul is in a text parallel to Col 2:7, in Eph 3:17. Whereas in Colossians we are rooted "in Christ," in the Ephesians parallel we are rooted "in love." This indicates for Paul that to be rooted in love is to be rooted in Christ who himself defines love, and to be rooted in love means that a person is necessarily rooted in Christ. The implication seems to be that apart from our corporate inclusion into the new man Jesus, we are deficient in regard to our ability to experience, enact, and receive love since our rooting in love is contingent upon our rootedness in Christ. Cf. George Montague T.S.M, *Growth in Christ: A Study in Saint Paul's Theology of Progress* (Fribourg: St. Paul's Press, 1961), 40.

[11]Lehrmann expresses this idea nicely in his koinonia ethics through the term "interrelatedness." Paul L. Lehrmann, *Ethics in a Christian Context* (London: SCM Press, 1963), 53. Cf. ibid., 55, 68, in which he describes the presence of Christ through the church as the "fellowship-creating relationship in which the 'one' confronts the 'other' in the maturing humanity of man." See also Gorman, *Cruciformity*, 161.

[12]This is powerfully stated in Montague, *Growth in Christ*, 159, quoting Wescott, who summarizes the teaching of Aquinas on this very point: "From Christ our head comes not only the increasing compactness of the members of the Church through faith, nor merely the connection or binding through the mutual help of charity, but certainly from him comes the members' actual operation or movement to action, according to the measure and ability of each member . . . for not only by faith is the mystical body compacted, nor merely by charity's connecting assistance does the body grow; but likewise *by the effectual composing activity springing from each member*, according to the measure of grace given him, and the actual motion to operation which God effects in us" (my emphasis).

[13]Ernest Best, *One Body in Christ: A Study in The Relationship of the Church to Christ in the Epistles of the Apostle Paul* (London: SPCK, 1955), 128. See also 138 on Col 2:19.

[14]On the theme of the "body of Christ" in Paul, see 1 Cor 10:16-17; 1 Cor 12; and Eph 4:1-16.

[15]The phrase "inhabiting the cruciform God" is a phrase I borrow here from Michael Gorman, who uses it as the title of his 2009 book *Inhabiting the Cruciform God.*

[16]Cf. Gal 3:27: "For as many of you as were baptized into Christ have put on Christ." See also Rom 13:14. Eph 4:24 "put on the new man" parallels Col 3:10 (my translation).

[17]The bond that leads to perfection (my view) is also held by Lohse, *Colossians,* 149: "It indicates result or purpose. Thus love is understood as the bond that leads to perfection. It binds together the members of the community who live in the unity of the 'body of Christ' . . . and thus produces 'perfection' in the community of the one body." Edward Lohse, *Colossians and Philemon: A Commentary on the Epistles to the Colossians and to Philemon* (Philadelphia: Fortress, 1971). See also Ernst Lohmeyer, *Die Briefe an die Philiper an die Kolosser und an Philemon* (Gottingen: Vandenhoeck & Ruprecht, 1964), 228. See also Sumney, *Colossians,* 219; Margaret Y. MacDonald, *Colossians and Ephesians* (Collegeville: Liturgical Press, 2000), 141; and Hans Hübner, *An Philemon, an die Kolosser, an die Epheser* (Tübingen: Mohr Siebeck, 1997), 106. Douglas J. Moo, *The Letters to the Colossians and to Philemon,* The Pillar New Testament Commentary Series (Grand Rapids: Eerdmans, 2008), 281-82, however, sees love as binding the virtues, which leads to perfection. Peter T. O'Brien, *Colossians, Philemon,* Word Biblical Commentary (Nashville: Thomas Nelson, 1982), 203, holds that it is the genitive of perfection, noting that this view is also held by De Plessis, Perfection, Percy, Schmauch, Lohse, Dibelius-Greeven, and Fridrichsen. James D. G. Dunn, *The Epistle to the Colossians and to Philemon: A Commentary on the Greek Text* (Grand Rapids: Eerdmans, 1996), 233, thinks it indicates result or purpose, which somewhat overlaps with my own view. See also Petr Pokorny, *Colossians: A Commentary,* trans. Siegfried S. Schatzmann (Peabody: Hendrickson Publishers, 1991), 172; Ceslaus Spicq O.P., *Agape in the New Testament, Volume Two: Agape in the Epistles of St. Paul, the Acts of the Apostles and the Epistles of St. James, St. Peter, and St. Jude,* trans. Sister Marie Aquinas McNamara, O.P. and Sister Mary Honoria Richter, O.P. (London: B. Herder, 1965), 66: "The word 'perfection' in the 'bond of perfection' refers to 'the bond that leads to perfection' and not to a 'perfect bond' (cf. Is 58:6; Acts 8:23). The thought is similar to Romans 13:10 and Galatians 5:14 where agape is said to fulfill and summarize all other precepts."

[18]Marshall McLuhan, *Understanding Media: The Extensions of Man* (New York: McGraw-Hill, 1964).

[19]Cf. 2 Cor 3:18, "And we all, with unveiled face, beholding the glory of the Lord, are being transformed into the same image from one degree of glory to another. For this comes from the Lord who is the Spirit." Also see 2 Cor 4:4-6:

In their case the god of this world has blinded the minds of the unbelievers, to keep them from seeing the light of the gospel of the glory of Christ, who is the image of God. For what we proclaim is not ourselves, but Jesus Christ as Lord, with ourselves as your servants for Jesus' sake. For God, who said, "Let light shine out of darkness," has shone in our hearts to give the light of the knowledge of the glory of God in the face of Jesus Christ.

6 AN APOLOGY FOR THE CHURCH

[1]See, e.g., 1 Cor 10:16; 12:27; and Eph 4:12 on the theme of the body of Christ; 1 Cor 3:16-17; 2 Cor 6:16; and Eph 2:21 on the theme of the church as the temple of the Holy Spirit; Gal 6:10; Eph 2:19; 1 Tim 3:5, 15; and 1 Pet. 4:17 on the theme of the church as the household of God; and 1 Tim 3:15 on the theme of the church as the pillar and fortress of truth.

[2]Can we delete this phrase from the lingo of modern evangelical church culture? We "do" chores, algebra, and the dishes; but *life* is not something we do as a task, rather, it is something we live as a journey and privilege. So let's stop being intentional about *doing* life, and instead be more hopeful, joyful, and intentionally joy-filled as we *live* it.

[3]Cf. Gal 5:6: "For in Christ Jesus neither circumcision nor uncircumcision counts for anything, but only faith which is energized (Gk. *energoumenē*) through love" (my translation). See also 2 Cor 3:18; Eph 4:20-24; and Col 3:9-10.

[4]Cyprian, Ep. 73:21, as cited in *Catechism of the Catholic Church* (Liguori: Liguori Publications, 1994), 224, CCC826.

[5]Russell Moore, "Adopted for Life, Ten Years Later: What I've Learned," July 27, 2012, Russell Moore (blog), www.russellmoore.com/2012/07/27/adopted-for-life-ten-years-later-what-ive-learned-since/.

[6]Samuel John Stone, "The Church's One Foundation," 1866.

7 WORSHIP AT THE KARAOKE CHAPEL

[1]The name of the pub and several characters in the story have been changed here out of respect for the privacy of individuals, but the events described here are completely true.

[2]For those uninitiated, or perhaps better, those undefiled, Frank Rizzo is the iconic, foul-mouthed character from the 1990s prank call team known as *The Jerky Boys*. He is famous for berating people in obscenity-laced tirades done in a classic Brooklyn accent.

[3]As Alexander Schmemann says regarding the church's propensity toward hijacking the art forms of the world and Christianizing them, "We do not realize that we never get anywhere because we never leave any place behind." Alexander Schmemann, *For the Life of the World: Sacraments and Orthodoxy* (Crestwood: St. Vladimir's Seminary Press, 1982), 28. In our quest to make church look just

like the world, and in our tendency to adopt a homogeneous church culture, we empty the church of its unique, revolutionary, and subversive countercultural force by forcing it into a mold of sameness and predictability.

[4]Jürgen Moltmann, *The Trinity and the Kingdom of God* (Minneapolis: Fortress Press, 1993), 58, 106.

8 How the Many Become One in Christ

[1]McGavran's publications, beginning with the 1955 release of *Bridges of God: A Study in the Strategy of Missions* (London: World Dominion Press, 1955) and later in the 1980 book *Understanding Church Growth* (Grand Rapids: Eerdmans, 1980), are recognized as the source of the HUP methodology.

[2]David Swanson, "Down with the Homogeneous Unit Principle? Can we call our church model 'biblical' if we're not reaching out to everyone?" *Leadership Journal Online*, August 2010, accessed December 22, 2015, www.christianitytoday.com/le/2010/august-online-only/down-with-homogeneous-unit-principle.html.

[3]McGavran, *Understanding Church Growth*, 85.

[4]McGavran notes that between 1958 and 1962, the Lutheran Church Missouri Synod had the most converts in Hong Kong because they identified and ministered to the most successful HUPs. He argues that if Anglicans and Baptists had "propagated the Gospel in those sections of society where the Lutherans were multiplying churches (there was abundant room for all) and had worked in the ways in which the Lutherans were working, they would not have been limited to a mere 100 percent or so per decade" (ibid., 87). Thus McGavran views mission as being carried out, ideally, only where successful people groups of homogeneous units can be identified.

[5]Ibid., 213: "In applying this principle, common sense must be assumed. The creation of narrow Churches, selfishly centered on the salvation of their own kith and kin only, is never the goal. Becoming Christians should never enhance tribal animosities or the arrogance which is so common to all human associations."

[6]Cf. Col 3:9-11, "Do not lie to one another, seeing that you have put off the old self with its practices and have put on the new self, which is being renewed in knowledge after the image of its creator. Here there is not Greek and Jew, circumcised and uncircumcised, barbarian, Scythian, slave, free; but Christ is all, and in all."

[7]E.g., in Rom 3:29-30, Paul writes: "Or is God the God of Jews only? Is he not the God of Gentiles also? Yes, of Gentiles also, since God is one—who will justify the circumcised by faith and the uncircumcised through faith."

[8]See especially Gal 2:11-14, where the issue at hand is clearly Peter's removal of himself from table fellowship with those believers who were not Jewish. This, and *not* an argument about works-righteousness and earning merit (contra Luther), frames the entire epistle. See also Eph 2:11-22, in which Paul proclaims

that although the Gentiles were once separated from the commonwealth of Israel, they have been brought near by the blood of Jesus, coreconciled with God and one another through the cross, and made at peace together as "one new man." Together they are fellow citizens, constituting the household of God (v. 19) and together growing as a "holy temple" as a "dwelling place for God by the Spirit" (v. 22). Thus the theme of the inclusion into the one people of God, globally and locally, is central not only to an *outworking* of the gospel for Paul but is *itself part of the gospel*. Again, this can be observed by Paul's comment about Peter's ethnocentric behavior as "not in step with the . . . gospel" (Gal 2:14). [9]Ps 71:4-6 states this:

> Rescue me, O my God, from the hand of the wicked,
>   from the grasp of the unjust and cruel man.
> For you, O Lord, are my hope,
>   my trust, O Lord, from my youth.
> Upon you I have leaned from before my birth;
>   you are he who took me from my mother's womb.
> My praise is continually of you.

See also Ps 22:9-11:

> Yet you are he who took me from the womb;
>   you made me trust you at my mother's breasts.
> On you was I cast from my birth,
>   and from my mother's womb you have been my God.
> Be not far from me,
>   for trouble is near,
>   and there is none to help.

And see also Ps 139:13-16:

> For you formed my inward parts;
>   you knitted me together in my mother's womb.
> I praise you, for I am fearfully and wonderfully made.
> Wonderful are your works;
>   my soul knows it very well.
> My frame was not hidden from you,
> when I was being made in secret,
>   intricately woven in the depths of the earth.
> Your eyes saw my unformed substance;
> in your book were written, every one of them,
>   the days that were formed for me,
>   when as yet there was none of them.

[10]This logic also applies to those in the church—across denominations—who dare to harm a child made in the image of God. For them, the justice of God awaits their assault on God through their assault on his children: "Whoever *assaults* one such child, *assaults me*, and he assaults not me but him who sent me. Whoever *physically abuses* one such child, *physically abuses* me, and he physically abuses not just me but him who sent me. Whoever *murders* one such child, *attempts to murder me*, and he attempts to murder not just me, but him who sent me" (my extrapolation of Mk 9:37).

[11]The same principle of inclusion applies to our welcoming embrace of elderly people, widowed people, and other peoples who are frequently excluded from church fellowship in the name of "church growth" and the HUP.

9 Cultivating a Counterculture of Cruciform Worship

[1]The major singles on that record were "Smells like Teen Spirit," "Come as You Are," "In Bloom," and "Lithium."

[2]For a great resource on the metrical psalms see Free Church of Scotland, *Sing Psalms: New Metrical Versions of the Book of Psalms* (Edinburgh: Free Church of Scotland, 2003).

[3]This is not meant as a slight against Hillsong. They've blessed the church with countless excellent worship songs. It is meant to critique the common desire by pastors and worship pastors to simply emulate Hillsong as a key to success.

[4]Billy Corgan, "Interview with Billy Corgan," interview by Monita Rajpal, *Talk Asia*, CNN, aired August 23, 2013, accessed December 22, 2015, http://edition.cnn .com/TRANSCRIPTS/1308/23/ta.01.html.

10 Introduction to Interpersonal Cruciformity

[1]Note: In Bostonian parlance, "kid" refers to any acquaintance regardless of age. In this case, we were both in our midtwenties.

[2]See BDAG for further lexical information on this word group. Walter Bauer, *A Greek-English Lexicon of the New Testament and Other Early Christian Literature*, 3rd ed., rev. and ed. Frederick William Danker, trans. W. F. Arndt and W. F. Gingrich, and augmented by F. W. Danker, 3rd ed (Chicago: University of Chicago Press, 2000), 861. See Mt 5:5; 11:29; 21:5. The related term *prautēs* is used as a virtue in 1 Cor 4:21; 2 Cor 10:1 ("the gentleness of Christ"); Gal 5:23; 6:1; Eph 4:2; Col 3:12; 2 Tim 2:25; Tit 3:2; Jas 1:21; 3:13; and 1 Pet 3:16.

[3]Peter Kreeft, *Back to Virtue: Traditional Moral Wisdom for Modern Moral Confusion* (San Francisco: Ignatius, 1992), 139.

11 Interpersonal Cruciformity in the Congregation

[1]The idea of critique as honesty comes from Mark Harris's talk at Worship Summit in the Spring of 2015 at Grand Canyon University.

[2]At the time I was actually an evangelical Christian but continued to serve in the Catholic church out of a friendship to the priest, and (unbeknownst to me at the time) a draw toward the historic liturgical Great Tradition of the church. The result of all of this culminated in my transition into evangelical Anglicanism in 2010 and my subsequent ordination to the diaconate and priesthood as an evangelical Anglican.

[3]I came into contact with the phrase "gracious intentionality" through a friend, Rev. Mark Booker, at Church of the Cross in Boston, Massachusetts.

13 THE LITURGY OF CRUCIFORM WORSHIP

[1]Emil Brunner, *Truth as Encounter* (Philadelphia: Westminster Press, 1964).

[2]Wolfgang Iser, *The Act of Reading: A Theory of Aesthetic Response* (Baltimore: Johns Hopkins University Press, 1980).

[3]Ibid., 137n4.

[4]Ibid., 9, 67. See also Wolfgang Iser, *Prospecting: From Reader Response to Literary Anthropology* (Baltimore: Johns Hopkins University Press, 1989), 17.

[5]Iser, *The Act of Reading*, 10: "Meaning is no longer an object to be defined but is an effect to be experienced."

[6]Ibid., 22 and 128, respectively.

[7]Cf. Brunner, *Truth as Encounter*, 132.

[8]Iser, *The Act of Reading*, 38.

[9]Ibid., 137.

[10]Ibid., 35.

[11]Ibid., 40.

[12]Brunner, *Truth as Encounter*, 176: "The word of Luther [was] that the Bible is the crib in which Christ lies." See also ibid., 132: "The tokens [doctrines] are not accidental to but necessarily connected with the content; without doctrine the content is non-existent for us. . . . Doctrine is certainly related instrumentally to the Word of God as token and framework, serving in relation to the reality— actual personal fellowship with God; but doctrine is indissolubly connected with the reality it represents."

[13]Cf. Iser, *The Act of Reading*, 140.

[14]Ibid., 127.

[15]Iser presents this concept of evoking and producing presence through ideation. He helpfully compares the phenomenon of disappointment that occurs when we see a film after having first read a novel. In the novel, he notes, we contribute through the act of reading and ideation to the construction of meaning and the presence of the characters. Often, when we see the film version after having read the book, we experience a discrepancy between, for example, the way we envisioned a particular character and the way the filmmakers portray the character. This often leads to a feeling of disappointment or disillusionment with

the film version brought about by the fact that the film version inserts passivity into the spot of activity and participation that is required for a book to generate meaning. He notes, "The real reason [that we feel let down] is that we have been excluded [from the creative act], and we resent not being allowed to retain the images which we had produced and which enabled us to be in the presence of our products as if they were real possessions" (ibid., 139).

[16]Brunner writes, "Jesus Christ himself, the One in whom God imparts himself to us, is called 'the Word.' It is therefore he, this Person, who really is the Word" (Brunner, *Truth as Encounter*, 132). Karl Barth articulates a very similar way of thinking about revelation in *Church Dogmatics I.1 The Doctrine of the Word of God* (London: Bloomsbury T&T Clark, 2010). See also Alister E. McGrath, *Christian Theology: An Introduction* (Oxford: Blackwell, 1994), 155 on Barth: "For Barth, the Bible is not itself revelation: it is a witness to revelation."

[17]This is particularly a problem for projects like the Jesus Seminar, which actually delete many biblical sayings and teachings of Jesus from the Bible on the grounds they are not authentic to the "Jesus of History."

[18]Some examples of these nonbiblical ideas are twenty-first-century fiscal conservatism, anti-immigration policies, and an obsession with the Second Amendment.

[19]The quintessential example of the macho-man-vengeance Christ (my words) can be observed in Mark Driscoll's 2007 *Relevant Magazine* article, in which he explains that "there is a strong drift toward the hard theological left. Some emergent types [want] to recast Jesus as a limp-wrist hippie in a dress with a lot of product in His hair, who drank decaf and made pithy Zen statements about life while shopping for the perfect pair of shoes. In Revelation, Jesus is a pride fighter with a tattoo down His leg, a sword in His hand and the commitment to make someone bleed. That is a guy I can worship. I cannot worship the hippie, diaper, halo Christ because I cannot worship a guy I can beat up." Mark Driscoll et. al., "7 Big Questions: Seven Leaders on where the Church is Headed," *Relevant Magazine* 24 (January-February 2007).

[20]This language of inhabiting the cruciform God is derived from both the title and the topic of Michael Gorman, *Inhabiting the Cruciform God: Kenosis, Justification, and Theosis in Paul's Narrative Soteriology* (Grand Rapids: Eerdmans, 2009).

14 THE CRUCIFORMATIONAL PRAYERS OF THE PEOPLE

[1]"Texts for Common Prayer," Anglican Church in North America, accessed August 20, 2016, http://anglicanchurch.net/?/main/texts_for_common_prayer.

[2]I find it amusing that churches often spend long periods of time inviting the Holy Spirit "in" to the worship event. I wonder if we forget, perhaps, that the Holy Spirit is already present in us, and that God himself by his Spirit is omni-

present. God is not a vampire that needs to be invited to our services. He's more than happy to sovereignly show up without our permission to change our lives and to change the world.

[3]Cf. Rom 12:2, in which Paul explicitly teaches that the renewal and transformation *of our minds* is intimately related to the knowledge of God's will which leads to good works. It is this very pattern that we earlier encountered in Paul's cruciformational theology in Colossians. See also 1 Pet 3:8.

15 THE CRUCIFORMATIONAL PREACHING AND SINGING OF THE WORD

[1]Alexander Schmemann, *For the Life of the World: Sacraments and Orthodoxy* (Crestwood: St. Vladimir's Seminary Press, 1982), 33.

[2]Wentzel Van Huyssteen captures this danger well when he writes: "A dominant theology, trusted by a group, may through ideologizing inject an element of uncritical dogmatism into a paradigm or conceptual model" and "trusted basic convictions may only too easily put a cloak of authority on conceptual models." Wentzel Van Huyssteen, *Theology and the Justification of Faith: Constructing Theories in Systematic Theology* (Grand Rapids: Eerdmans; 1989), 64-65.

[3]Even the most conservative and revered of Reformed theologians, Charles Hodge, is aware that exalting doctrinal systems to a place of irreformable, untouchable hermeneutical pride of place is unacceptable and counterproductive. He writes in his *Systematic Theology*, "Theologians are not infallible in the interpretation of Scripture. It may, therefore, happen in the future, as it has in the past, that interpretations of the Bible, long confidently received, must be modified or abandoned, *to bring revelation into harmony with what God teaches in his word.* This change of view as to the true meaning of the Bible may be a painful trial to the Church, but it does not in the least impair the authority of the Scriptures. They remain infallible; we are merely convicted of having mistaken their meaning." Charles Hodge, *Systematic Theology* (Grand Rapids: Eerdmans, 1975), as used in Gary L. W. Johnson and Ronald N. Gleason, *Reforming or Conforming? Post-Conservative Evangelicals and the Emerging Church* (Wheaton: Crossway, 2008), 141 (my emphasis).

[4]Christopher Boyd Brown, *Singing the Gospel: Lutheran Hymns and the Success of the Reformation* (Boston: Harvard University Press, 2005), 10-11.

[5]Ibid., 65, 76.

[6]John R. Tyson, *Assist Me to Proclaim: The Life and Hymns of Charles Wesley* (Grand Rapids: Eerdmans, 2007), vii-viii.

[7]Jeremy Pierce as quoted in Justin Taylor, "Annoying Things in Worship, Songs" from The Gospel Coalition (blog), February 11, 2014, accessed December 28, 2015, http://blogs.thegospelcoalition.org/justintaylor/2014/02/11/annoying-things-in-worship-songs/.

16 CRUCIFORMATION THROUGH HOLY COMMUNION

[1]Scott Hahn, *Consuming the Word: The New Testament and the Eucharist in the Early Church* (New York: Image, 2013), 22, states, "In Jesus' only use of the term, we find that 'New Testament' refers not to a text, but to a rite and to the new order brought about by means of that rite." Also, "What the first Christians knew as the 'New Testament' was not a book, but the Eucharist," and "He [Jesus] called his action the 'new covenant in my blood' (Luke 22:20). He declared it to be the New Testament—and the Testament was not a text but an action. He did not say 'read this' or 'write this' but rather 'do this.'" (ibid., 39). "The New Testament was a sacrament at least a generation before it was a document. We learn this from the document itself" (ibid., 40).

[2]Mk 8:6, "And he directed the crowd to sit down on the ground. And he took the seven loaves, and having given thanks [Gk. *Eucharisteō*], he broke (*klaō*) them and gave them to his disciples to set before the people; and they set them before the crowd." The verbal form here is literally "having eucharisted" ["having given thanks"] he broke the bread. Cf. Mt 15:36/Mk 8:6 the feeding of the four thousand.

17 CRUCIFORMISSION

Epigraph: Alexander Schmemann, *For the Life of the World: Sacraments and Orthodoxy* (Crestwood: St. Vladimir's Seminary Press, 1982), 36-37.

[1]The idea of the church as a "contradiction" to the present world order is a frequent theme in Jürgen Moltmann, *Theology of Hope: On the Ground and the Implications of a Christian Eschatology* (Minneapolis: Fortress Press, 1993). See, e.g., 21. The term "holy troublemakers" is a term that finds its roots in Shane Claiborne's writing about the living out of the revolutionary love of Jesus. He beautifully captures the heart of Moltmann's idea of contradicting the world when he notes the following:

> I grew up thinking that being a good Christian was synonymous with being a good, churchgoing, middle-class, well-behaved American. But as you take a closer look at church history, you can't miss the fact that some of the greatest saints and prophets have been holy troublemakers, instigators and agitators, prophetic pranksters and grace-filled revolutionaries—folks who disturb the status quo because they do not accept the world as it is but insist that another world is possible and devote their lives to seeing that would come to be, on earth as it is in heaven.

Shane Claiborne, "Divine Rebels: American Christian Activists for Social Justice," *Huff Post Religion*, April 27, 2011, accessed on December 29, 2015, www.huffingtonpost.com/shane-claiborne/divine-rebels-american-ch_b_852468.html.

[2]Moltmann, *Theology of Hope*, 21.

[3]Ibid., 288.

[4]I am borrowing the phrase "gospel inertia" from Shane Claiborne. I've been using it since my interview with Shane for the global Ecclesia and Ethics conference at which Shane gave an address. See University of St. Andrews, "Ecclesia and Ethics Interview Shane Claiborne—2/5/2013," February 7, 2013, accessed January 14, 2016, www.youtube.com/watch?v=XJ47ChxmXqY.

[5]According to 2 Cor 5:14-21, since we have been reconciled through Christ (v. 18a) we are now given the "ministry of reconciliation" (v. 18b) in which God calls us to be "ambassadors for Christ" (v. 20) for the reconciliation of the world to God and one another through Christ (vv. 20-21). Thus I like to refer to our reality and vocation in Christ as that of being "reconciled reconcilers." The ones whom God has reconciled to himself become the means by which God reconciles the world to himself. The agency, vocation, and mission of the church is not simply incidental and peripheral to the reconciliation of all things. Rather, the church is the body, mechanism, instrument, and agent by which God effects redemption in the world (see also Col 1:19-22). On reshaping the world, see Moltmann, *Theology of Hope*, 330: Christians are called to live in "practical opposition to the way things are, and in creative reshaping of them."

[6]Shane Claiborne, "Ask Shane Claiborne . . . (Response)," Rachel Held Evans (blog), February 27, 2013, accessed December 29, 2015, http://rachelheldevans .com/blog/ask-shane-claiborne-response.

[7]Jürgen Moltmann, *The Future of Creation: Collected Essays* (Philadelphia: Fortress Press, 1979), 122.

AUTHOR INDEX

SUBJECT INDEX

SCRIPTURE INDEX